PRAISE FOR BET

D1040110

▶ "Wow, this book is breathtaking! Sadi̇ tragedy rises humanity and unexpected heroes and heroines." **David Estes**, bestselling author of *The Fatemarked Epic* series

▶ "Heartrending and inspiring. Sadie is a modern day warrior in the battle against pediatric cancer, and her story will leave you hopeful for the future." **Melanie Conklin**, author of *Counting Time*

▶ "Nobody wants to think about child cancer, but we can't look away. Our children deserve better. This fierce, heartbreaking book had me cheering, crying, and ultimately shouting *You got this girl!* The strength of Sadie Keller, and the children like her, shines through on every page and will stay with you long after you close the book." **Wendy Mills**, award-winning author of *Positively Beautiful*

▶ "*Better Angels* is so inspiring and deeply personal, you can feel the honesty and emotion coming off the pages." **Amanda Maxlyn**, *USA Today* bestselling author

▶ "This is a book about hope. As a survivor who courageously endured childhood cancer treatment, Sadie's insights and experience are particularly meaningful. Her work with Congress to help bring cures to children, not just in America but around the world, is compelling." **David G. Poplack, M.D.**, Professor of Pediatric Oncology, Baylor College of Medicine; Director, Global HOPE, Texas Children's Hospital

▶ "Sadie Keller shares her inspirational story of confronting cancer with grace, courage, and humor. Her vibrant, compelling account reminds us all of the importance of our work in the lab and the clinic to do better for all of our patients. We are proud to join her in Making Cancer History." **Jim Allison, Ph.D.**, Winner of the Nobel Prize for Medicine and Chair of Immunology at University of Texas MD Anderson Cancer Center

▶ "When Sadie Keller was diagnosed with cancer at age seven, she worked with her family and a member of Congress to bring hope and new treatments to children struggling with the disease. Her optimism and strength in the face of adversity are an inspiration." **Michael Dell**, Founder and CEO of Dell Technologies and benefactor of Dell Children's Medical Center of Central Texas

Better Angels

You can change the world.
You are not alone.

SADIE KELLER
with MICHAEL McCAUL

Published by Gavia Books

Paperback ISBN 978-0-9978808-5-4
Hardcover ISBN 978-0-9978808-6-1

Library of Congress Control Number 2020902349

The events and conversations in this book have been set down to the best of the author's ability, although some names and details have been changed to protect the privacy of individuals.

More information on the Sadie Keller Foundation can be found at
SadieKellerFoundation.org

Cover art by Sadie Keller | Book design by Tessa Avila

Second printing September 2020
Printed with soy inks
Printed in the United States of America

for **Lily**

and all the other angels

Contents

Contents

Grab My Hands and Look Up

I was sitting in my office, getting ready for a television interview, when the lobbyist walked in. She was eight years old and hardly stood taller than the edge of my desk. Wearing a pink dress and a band on her hairless head, she carried nothing more than her story.

But I'll tell you, it's a heck of a story.

We had met before, when I saw her give a short speech in front of a cheering crowd, and I knew she was an eloquent voice for her cause. So I asked her to join me in the interview, about passing a law to bring more state-of-the-art care to children with cancer. She told a very short version of her story—scary and heartbreaking, triumphant and inspiring.

Every cancer kid, and every cancer kid's family, has their own story to tell. I don't know anyone who tells it better than Sadie Keller.

That afternoon, I canceled the rest of my appointments and showed Sadie around the U.S. Capitol Building. When you meet Sadie—and you will in the pages that follow—you realize she's the kind of person you want to make the rest of the day for: smart and funny and brave and generous, completely honest, and yet a perfectly ordinary little girl.

Except.

She went through what she calls the Hard Time—one where she lost close friends to cancer—and came out wanting nothing more than to help other children. Then she joined forces with organizations that carry the power of their own stories. At a time when you think nothing useful can get done in government, when the country seems completely divided, when you think that nothing but money drives whatever goes on in Washington, you just need to listen to Sadie.

The really good news: It's leading to laws being passed that spell hope for the children of America and may even save the lives of children around the world.

That afternoon, I led Sadie through the Capitol down to the Rotunda, the dome in the heart of the building.

"Hey," I said. "If you look up and spin around, you'll get really dizzy." I held out my hands and she took them. We walked right into the physical heart of our democracy, looked up, and spun. People stood around and watched us. It felt like dancing.

It still does.

Michael McCaul

Better Angels

CHAPTER ONE

Find the Angels

can't speak. The words sit in my brain and won't come out.

It started earlier in the day, only not with my mouth. We picked up chicken tenders at Whataburger in the afternoon, and when I went to grab my food, my right arm just fell on the table. I lifted it up with my other hand to pick up my chicken tender, and it dropped again. Once I started eating, my arm started to feel weird. Mom called the doctor, who said to keep an eye on it. Then my arm felt better and I forgot about it.

That evening, I'm at home with Grandma while Mom and Dad are at my brother's football game. We bake a cake, huge and round with two tiers, and wait for the others to come home.

"Sadie, it's getting late," Grandma says. "Should we eat?"

"No, I want to wait." But the words don't come out right. I'm having trouble saying it. My mouth won't move the way I wanted, and my tongue can't match up with the sounds. But Grandma doesn't notice.

I go into Mom's bathroom and call her, panicking. "Are you at Grant's game?"

"Yeah."

"I'm really having trouble saying words."

Mom starts walking out of the game even while she's talking to me. She and Dad had driven there in separate cars. "Hold on," she says. "I'm on my way."

I hang up and tell Grandma about my trouble saying words.

She pats the couch next to her. "Sit. Let's do tongue twisters." She has me say, "How much wood could a woodchuck chuck if a woodchuck could chuck wood."

"Ow uch ood coo a wood...."

"She sells seashells by the seashore."

"She shells... I can't!!" My face feels tingly. I can't think straight. Every word comes out crooked and with a lot of effort.

Grandma takes me upstairs to pack a bag for the hospital. Mom had called the on-call doctor even before driving home: "I think she's having a stroke!" When she gets home, she yells, "Sadie!" I start running downstairs, bawling.

"Where are you going?" Grandma asks. She didn't hear Mom.

"Myyyy om heaw." My mom's here.

We don't even grab my bag. I'm crying hard, and Mom is scared out of her mind. She picks me up in her arms and carries me to the car. During the 45-minute drive to the hospital, Mom keeps reaching back and patting me.

A neurologist—a doctor who specializes in brains and nerves—is waiting for me. "Squeeze my fingers as hard as you can." I try but can barely make any pressure. It's like I'm telling my body to do things, but it isn't listening.

"What's your name?"

It takes a while to say, "...Sadie Keller."

"Where are you?"

"......I'm in the hospital."

"Can you say, 'Remember'?"

"Ruhmema."

The doctor runs tests for a brain bleed, then puts me in a giant scary MRI machine for more than half an hour to measure any brain damage. They don't find anything.

I'm not having a stroke. But I had been poisoned. On purpose.

The poison had gotten rid of the cancer, leukemia, that had invaded my blood. It let me live by poisoning the cancer, killing the runaway cells that are what cancer is all about. My family and I, our neighbors and friends and everybody, had celebrated when I had gone into remission—when the doctors couldn't find any more cancer cells in my body. But even after remission, the doctors kept dripping that poison into a hole in my chest. This was to last for two and a half years. Now that same medicine was taking away my words—just for a while, but it would happen a second time.

Still, I found my voice. It turned out to be a bigger voice than I ever thought possible.

Besides, things could have been much worse for me and my family. When you have childhood cancer, you make a lot of friends who go through the same thing. Unlike my friends at school, these friends are in danger. Cancer is the number one disease killing children. I made many friends among cancer kids, and I lost some of them—some of my closest friends.

But my story isn't about dying. It's about finding your voice, even when that's a struggle. I hope you read my

4

story even if you have never had cancer and don't know any kid who has had it.

This is a story that doesn't end. Some of the effects of my cancer treatment will last for the rest of my life. I'll make more friends among kids with cancer and will do what I can to make them happier. And the odds are, some of them will fight until they can't fight anymore. They'll leave behind family and friends with broken hearts.

My story isn't like most of the stories you read or the ones in the movies. Those have a neat ending: the girl wins the throne, the children break the icy spell, the lion cub grows up and takes over the pride. Most stories in real life, though, don't end. Mine won't either. Honestly, I don't want it to, because here is what I learned:

In the worst of times, you need to keep a good heart and look for the angels. They're all around you. If you welcome them, and let them help, if you keep your faith that all this is happening for a reason—even if it all seems crazy and terrible—then a miracle can happen. The miracle is this: What seems like a curse becomes a blessing.

Find the angels, and they will help you find the blessing.

I'm living proof. The angels in my life include my parents and brother Grant, who made me laugh even when they wanted to cry. They include my amazing oncologist and my child life specialist and nurses who said and did all the right things and taught me more about cancer than I ever would have wanted to know. They include our neighbors in our little community of Lantana, Texas, where people keep track of each other and help in times of trouble.

They include a Member of Congress, Michael McCaul, a powerful man who became my friend almost as if we were the same age, and who let me help him get a childhood cancer bill passed and signed by the President. And they include the kids I met in the hospital and clinic, who shared stories and played with me even while they were going through the Hard Time themselves.

All of them are angels. A few are in Heaven. This book is dedicated to them.

Sadie

CHAPTER TWO

Mama? Am I Going to Die?

The news came two months before my birthday. But what was wrong happened before that.

I was a soccer player. On fall weekends I would wake up early to go to a soccer game, where all my friends were my teammates. Then, during one game, I was running after the ball and suddenly it hurt to breathe. Gasping for air, I slowed to a walk. You know that feeling when you run really fast and then have to stop to catch your breath? It was like that, only I couldn't catch my breath. Even standing still, my body felt like it was still running as fast as it could.

"Sadie!" My coach ran onto the field. "Are you okay?"

I wasn't. I was crying, freaking out because I couldn't breathe, and being scared doesn't exactly help you breathe.

The coach took me to my mom on the sidelines, and she calmed me down a bit, but I still felt really tired. My legs hurt. They were clamped tight, like they would collapse under me and break. My stomach clenched.

This wasn't like me. I was a fast soccer player, always going after the ball and passing it to my friends so they could get a goal. Whenever the ball was in a huddle of girls, I pushed in to kick it out. I love winning. And now I couldn't even finish the game.

After five minutes or so, I caught my breath and drank some water. My muscles ached. I felt like I had run a marathon. The other kids kept looking my way whenever they ran past. *What's going on?* I hate being looked at like that.

I had no idea that, within a few months, people would be staring at me a whole lot more. And not in a good way.

More un-Sadie-like things happened. I never used to get sick, but that winter I got the flu with a high fever and had to miss school for four days. A couple weeks later, I got strep throat with another high fever. The doctor put me on antibiotics, and after a few more days at home, I went back to school.

One night, when I was still on antibiotics, I was taking a bath. Mom was in the bathroom with me. I went to wash my legs and noticed something weird: These tiny red dots covered both my thighs. They looked like polka dots.

Huh.

"Mom, what are these?"

"Do they itch?"

"No."

No big deal, we figured.

The next day at school, I went to the bathroom and lifted my shirt and found the polka dots all over my stomach. Again, I didn't make a big deal of it and didn't tell anyone until Mom picked me up after school.

"The dots are all over my stomach now."

"Lift up your shirt."

Polka dot extravaganza.

"Huh," she said. "Maybe you're having a reaction to the antibiotic." She called the doctor's office and made an appointment for the next day. When the nurse took my temperature, the thermometer read 99.9 degrees. "Low grade fever," she said.

The doctor agreed with Mom that I might be having a reaction to the antibiotic and told Mom to watch me.

Which would be easy to do: That same day we were driving to visit my grandparents, Mimi and Pop, in San Antonio.

Pop, my grandfather, took one look at me and said to Mom, "Is Sadie feeling okay? She looks really pale."

The next day, my Aunt Amy came over. She lives near my Mimi and Pop, Mom's parents. "Why is Sadie green?" she asked.

"I'm green?"

Aunt Amy kept talking to Mom. "Is she about to throw up? Does she have a stomach bug?"

"I feel fine!" I said.

Soon after, we all went down to River Walk. It's my favorite part of San Antonio, a place filled with flowers and shops and restaurants along the river. I've strolled up and down it tons of times. But this time I started fussing. "I can't walk anymore."

My parents weren't happy with me. They wanted me to walk.

"I can't!"

Dad finally put me on his shoulders.

We drove home early from San Antonio to beat a huge ice storm. When we got back, I noticed more dots on my wrist, even though I was off antibiotics. Mom called the pediatrician, who answered the phone herself. No one else could get to work that Monday because of the ice.

"Let's bring her in for bloodwork," the doctor said. "You won't be able to get there today. Try going tomorrow. And then let's make a follow-up appointment on Thursday."

My friend Cameron kept me company to the place where they draw blood. A phlebotomist, the person who gets the blood, took me back into a small room where the blood chair is. She told me to put my arm out straight. I was scared. She gave me a colorful teddy bear, and Cameron and I counted all the colors on it.

At school the next day, I wondered whether the dots on my wrist could let me skip class and go to the nurse, just for fun. The nurse would give me a peppermint, and I'd go back to class. It would be a great break. I went up to the teacher and told her I had a rash on my wrist, thinking she would send me to the nurse. Instead, she just gave me some lotion. So much for getting out of class.

But right after that, I was in computer lab, trying to learn how to type (I'm terrible at it), when my teacher called me out of the room. "Sadie, you're leaving for the day."

"What? I just got back!"

I walked to the office and saw Mom standing there. I raised my arms like, *What's the story?*

She smiled. "Hey, how's your day?"

"Short," I said.

Mom told me we were going back to the doctor.

"Why? We were just there."

"The results are in," she said. Mom didn't tell me until later that this time it was a much bigger deal. That morning, the pediatrician had tried to call her but had an old number, so the doctor called my dad.

"Are Sarah and Sadie with you?" the doctor asked Dad. "We got Sadie's lab results back and something's wrong. I'm sending you guys to Children's Medical Center in Dallas."

Dad called Mom. "I'm trying to keep it together here," he said. "I just got a call from Dr. Butler. She said something's wrong with Sadie's blood. I'm already on my way."

Mom started to cry. She grabbed her shoes and drove to the school.

On our way to the doctor, she called a neighbor and I could hear her crying and I started to get scared.

Dad was already at the pediatrician's when we got there. The three of us went into the examining room, and I sat on Mom's lap. The doctor was holding papers. "We got Sadie's lab results back," she said. "They show that she has acute leukemia. It's cancer."

Dad grabbed Mom's hand, and Mom hugged me so tight it was hard to breathe. Tears blurred my eyes. I whispered into Mom's ear: "Mama? Am I going to die?" Cancer. That's what happens, right? You get cancer and you die?

"No, Baby," she said. "No. You're going to be all right."

"Go home and pack your bags," the doctor said. "Then get to the hospital by three. You're probably going to be there for a couple of weeks."

Mom was like, *We can't get there fast enough.* She picked my brother, Grant, up from school so we could all be together, then everybody went into action mode. I could see they were trying to hold it together, but they were super scared.

Before I packed, I found a piece of paper and a green marker and wrote:

Dear Mom and Dad and Grant,
Everything's going to be fine as long as we're together.
Love, Sadie

And I got a little wooden cross and stuck it under Mom and Dad's bedsheets.

Then I took out my pink cheetah print bag, a duffel I've had for many years, and collected photographs from around the house of me and my family. I probably should have been thinking of clothes and toiletries and that sort of thing, but I was scared. This would be my first night ever in a hospital. Would it be a tiny room with a white bed and an IV pole like in the movies? Would my family be allowed with me? Could they sit on my bed and talk? I hate being by myself without my mom.

All this was terrifying, but I learned later that we were actually lucky. A lot of kids get diagnosed in the emergency room. *Boom! Guess what? You have cancer!* The doctor tells you and your parents in this crazy place where it's really busy, and they often can't spend too much time letting you all process the news. Plus, the most common age for my kind of cancer is three to five. These are very little kids. I was little, but not *that* little. I could understand the news.

Mom came in and helped me pack pajamas and comfortable clothes. Then we all got in the car and drove 45 minutes to the hospital in Dallas. We got off the elevator on the sixth floor. The sign said:

WELCOME TO CHILDRENS MEDICAL CENTER
ONCOLOGY FLOOR AND BLOOD DISORDERS

Blood disorders?

It was a busy place with signs everywhere, INTAKE this way, CLINIC this way, INPATIENTS that way. I would end up knowing all of them all too well. Nurses and doctors rushed by, and there were families with their kids. A lot of the children were bald. Was I going to lose my hair? There were kids holding IV poles, walking with a line attached to their chest. I saw tubes, and nurses walking with them, and more nurses sprinting down the hallway the way they do on TV when someone's dying. Kids were sitting on the clinic side. A lot of them looked pale and tired and sat like they had been there forever.

Would I have to stay here forever?

I saw another sign:

Pauline Allen Gill Center for
Cancer and Blood Disorders

Cancer. It said CANCER right there on the wall. It took me by surprise, even though we had already heard the news about me. This was getting real.

We checked in at the front desk, and they put a hospital bracelet on my wrist and sent me into Intake. There they took my height and weight and temperature, and across the hall they drew my blood again. I was teary-eyed

14

and my heart was beating really fast and I was *terrified* of needles. The phlebotomist who took my blood was named Fatima, a really nice woman with long curly hair. She wore red scrubs. She still takes my blood, and she's one of my best friends today. But that first time I didn't know how often I'd be there.

I sat on Mom's lap and put out my arm. Fatima took the cap off a needle. She asked me, "Do you want me to count?"

"Yes." It goes faster when the phlebotomist does a countdown, and it makes you not jump in surprise and mess it up. But I was shaking.

Fatima took an orange elastic band and tied it around my upper arm so she could get the vein where she could see it. My arm started tingling, and she put the needle in and it hurt a little bit. But I had already done it a couple days before, and I knew it wouldn't hurt that bad. She got the blood, took the needle out, put a piece of gauze on, then placed a Band-Aid on top of that.

I couldn't have known it then, but in the next couple of years I would get blood taken out of me more than 250 times.

A nurse took us to a clinic room, and I sat on the examining table. Two ladies were already there. "I'm Dr. Engel," said one. She was wearing a suit and a stethoscope. "I'm your oncologist." (That's not her real name. I changed it to protect her privacy. *Engel* means angel in German.) She shook all our hands. I learned later that an oncologist is a cancer doctor. Dr. Engel is also a hematologist, someone who diagnoses blood problems. I was glad she didn't tell me that at the time. I was still a little freaked out by the phlebotomist.

"And I'm Caitlin." A woman in her twenties with light brown hair, she was wearing scrub pants and a tee shirt. She said she was a certified child life specialist. Dr. Engel and Caitlin would be with me through the Hard Time for the next two and a half years and beyond.

Caitlin smiled at me. "Sadie, would you and Grant like to come with me to another room?"

I didn't want to. I was scared about leaving Mom and Dad. But I hate to upset people, and I usually say yes even when I want to say no. So my brother and I went to another clinic room that looked just like the first one. Caitlin brought out a big fabric doll about the size of a toddler, along with a sort of tackle box, like the kind people use for lures when they go fishing. The doll was bald.

She asked Grant and me some questions—what was our favorite color, what did we do for fun, that sort of thing. Then she said, "I work with kids like y'all. And I'm going to explain what's happening to your body, and what will happen."

She stood the doll up. It had a little hole at the top of its chest, below the neck. A little plastic lump lay under the fabric. "This is a port," she said. "Want to feel it?"

We felt it: just a bump.

She said, "You access the port with a little needle." She took out a butterfly needle—a little pin with handles that look like wings. She put it into the doll. "You need to clean it first for 30 seconds and let it dry for 15 seconds, and all the germs will go away." She pulled the needle out. "This is the needle that goes into your veins so that all your medicine can go into your body."

Wait. A needle? In my chest? *That goes in a lot of the time?* "Can you feel it going in?" My voice shook.

"Well," she said, "they numb it up so when the needle goes in you can't feel it at all." She took out a folder with pictures of what a port looks like and how they stick it under your skin with surgery. "This way you don't have to get poked every single time you go in for your chemo— the medicine you'll be getting to make you better."

Okay, that sounded a little better. It's not like you get stuck with a needle in your arm. But wait. *Surgery???* I had never had surgery before. This was more terrifying than anything else I had heard so far that day.

"When?"

Caitlin raised her eyebrows.

"When is the..."

"The surgery? Tomorrow."

I felt a little faint and leaned into Grant.

Caitlin then explained what leukemia is. She took out a red tube, a giant version of a vein with bone marrow in it. She told Grant and me about red blood cells and platelets. "The chemo kills all your cancer cells so you're healthy again. You might need blood and platelets some-times. They come in a bag and through your port to keep your body strong and healthy."

This was a bunch of information on things I didn't know anything about. It was like school, and I sat there just listening the way you do with a teacher. But honestly, I missed a lot of it. I was only seven. Grant was ten years old and understood better. But a couple of things stuck with me:

1. *I'm going to have to get bags of blood!!*
2. *I'm having surgery...tomorrow!!!*

Then she said something else that stayed with me: "It's not your fault. You didn't do anything to cause this cancer."

Mom and Dad told me later that, while we were with Caitlin—it was more than an hour—Dr. Engel was saying the same thing to them, only in grownup terms. Unlike a lot of adult cancers, leukemia in children seems to be just an accident. "Childhood cancer happens because their bodies are growing fast, and their cells are multiplying," Dr. Engel told them. "Along the way, their body just makes a mistake."

It starts with white blood cells, the body's main soldiers. Doctors call them leucocytes. They're the largest cells found in your blood, like big-muscled war fighters. When bad germs or viruses attack, the white blood cells run toward them and destroy them. They're a good thing, usually. Your body needs them to stay healthy.

Usually, white blood cells are supposed to multiply and die, multiply and die. They multiply by making exact copies of themselves. But with leukemia, something goes wrong: One of the cells doesn't get copied right. While the first cell dies, the bad copy doesn't know it's supposed to die. Then it copies itself, and that copy doesn't know *it's* supposed to die. And both cells keep copying and copying with cells that don't die, totally out of control. And those are the cancer cells.

It's weird when you think about it that way. Cancer is a horrible disease, and we're all scared of it. But all childhood leukemia is, is cells—good cells, which you need to live—that don't know how to die. Like they never read the manual.

Those crazy leukemia cells kill one out of every five kids who get them in this country. Which meant I had four chances in five of surviving this. Nobody told me that then. It may seem like good odds to you. And compared to Africa, where nine out of ten kids with leukemia die, we Americans are lucky. But don't tell that to the parents.

Dr. Engel explained to Mom and Dad what was going to happen to me. "There are different kinds of leukemia," she said. "We know Sadie has leukemia, but we don't know specifically what kind she has. So we'll do a bone marrow biopsy."

A biopsy is when they take a piece out of you and study it. In this case, they draw out some of the stuff that's in the middle of your bone, the marrow, which is bright red with red and white blood cells. The plan was for Dr. Engel to do the biopsy while the surgeon put a port into my chest. "We're going to tag team it while she's under anesthesia," she said. She was also going to do a spinal tap, pulling fluid out of my spine. "And I'm going to give her the first dose of chemo into her spinal fluid in case the cancer is in there."

The biopsy would tell what kind of cancer it was. There are two main kinds of leukemia: ALL and AML. The first, acute lymphoblastic leukemia, is the more common one. Dr. Engel said if I had ALL, I would have to get chemo for about two and a half years but wouldn't have to stay in the hospital all that time. If the bone marrow showed I had AML, acute myeloid leukemia, the time for chemo would be shorter—six to nine months. But I would have to be in the hospital for almost all that time.

Mom was thinking, *Which one should we hope it is? If it's ALL, Sadie will be Grant's age by the time they finish. If it's AML, she'll be stuck in this hospital.* Neither one sounded great. "When will we get the results of the biopsy?" Mom asked.

"Final results in a few days," Dr. Engel said. "But we should get the basic results a few hours after surgery."

Surgery. Tomorrow.

CHAPTER THREE

Stop...Crying!

D ad pulled a wagon full of our overnight stuff to our hospital room. It was what I had imagined: all white, no color. There were windows along the whole back wall, with a view of downtown Dallas. Underneath the windows was a small blue plastic loveseat. There was a bed of course, with an IV pole next to it. Not at all like what a kid's room should be.

We put our stuff down, and I lay in the bed. A nurse put a needle into the top of my right hand with a tube that went into a vein. Every time I moved my hand—which was a lot, since I move my hands when I talk—I could feel the tube moving, and it hurt. Plus the bed was uncomfortable, with a mattress as hard as a rock. The sheets scratched my skin. They were like sandpaper. The blankets were scratchy and thin.

Mom went down to the gift shop and got me a little brown Teddy bear. It's the softest thing, with a floppy neck, and I still sleep with it. I really needed that bear. From when we got into the room at 3:30 in the afternoon until midnight, nurses kept coming in and out. They took my vitals and told me the plan: I was getting two whole bags of blood to help bring my red blood cell count back up. A nurse hung one bag, and it took two hours to empty into me. Then she switched bags for another two hours. The blood bags are clear, and the blood looks like...blood. These bags seemed too big to put all that blood into one little girl. I thought, *All that is going into my body?*

And then I thought, *That's somebody else's blood.* When I think about that today, I realize how cool it was that

22

someone, a total stranger, helped save me. You never see all the angels.

Meanwhile, Grant sat on the bed with me, and we watched some shows on his phone. Balloons and stuffed animals started pouring into the room from friends at school, our neighbors, our family, and even from some people I didn't know.

Word was spreading. One reason was Kelly, a woman who worked at the front desk in my elementary school. When Mom went to pick up Grant while I was packing for the hospital, Kelly saw her crying. Mom told Kelly I had cancer. And word spreads fast in our neighborhood. Kelly's son, Kincaid, had a brain tumor, and he was having his last chemo when I was admitted. His sister, Maddie, sent me a fluffy stuffed dog, along with some balloons.

In the hospital room, Dad and Grant stepped out for a while. Mom sat in a chair next to my bed while I watched a movie on TV. She called our neighbor, Miss Stephanie, to bring her up to speed. Something—maybe the sound of a sniffle—made me look from the TV over at Mom. Tears were coming down her face while she talked about me and cancer. I pointed my finger at her, raised my eyebrows, and mouthed so Miss Stephanie couldn't hear:

STOP...CRYING!

Mom got it. I needed her to be strong. I was ready to fight, but I needed her to fight with me. Mom knew that when she looked afraid, I would be afraid. When she seemed sad, I got sad. Even now I hate seeing Mom or Dad cry. That means I need to be sad. Which makes me nervous. If anybody cries, I get nervous.

So when I told her silently to stop crying, Mom dried her tears. She hung up and took a deep breath. *Okay,* she thought. *Let's do this.*

In the three years since that night, I've thought a lot about bravery. Soldiers are brave, obviously, and you have to be brave when a nurse comes at you with a needle. But a mother not letting her little girl see tears when that girl just might die? That must be one of the bravest things of all. From then on, Mom saw scary things, disgusting things, she saw me in pain, she saw lab reports that were bad news, she saw me when steroids made me crazy and when I was in pain and when I felt stuck, like, forever in the hospital; and she smiled and looked cheerful the whole time she was around me.

Which was not only brave. It was really good acting.

That first night in the hospital we all ordered dinner from the cafeteria. I had spaghetti and curly fries. I didn't like the food; I'm a picky eater. My favorite lunch is turkey on a sub roll. The turkey has to be Oscar Mayer, and the roll has to be a special kind of roll, and definitely not sliced bread. My favorite dinner is buttered rice. Still, I ate the spaghetti and fries. I skipped dessert, even though I usually like dessert.

Grant and Dad left at ten o'clock, and I got my pajamas on. The nurses kept coming. At midnight they started me on platelets, having put up another big bag filled with a thick, opaque liquid this disgusting yellow puke color, like pea soup. Which, I don't have to tell you, I don't like. The platelets started flowing from the bag down the tube and into the vein in my hand. As it traveled all the way into me, I instantly started feeling itchy everywhere on my body, as if a thousand mosquitoes were all biting me at once. I started scratching my arm, then my leg, then my chest and stomach.

Mom was sitting next to me in bed. "What's the matter?"

"I'm really itchy!"

A nurse was standing at a computer in the corner of the room, checking my vitals. She came over.

"My face feels weird," I said. "And my tongue. Let me see a mirror."

Mom looked at me. My face was swelling up so much that she could barely recognize me. Not wanting me to freak out, she didn't hand me a mirror.

The nurse said, "She's having an allergic reaction to the platelets." She unplugged the line into my hand. "I'm going to get some Benadryl and Tylenol."

My eyes swelled shut. I could barely see.

The nurse came back with a doctor, an on-call fellow. He looked me over while the nurse put the medicine in my IV. I felt better right away, though it took a while for the swelling to go down. The nurse said, "From now on we'll pre-medicate with Benadryl and Tylenol before giving platelets."

But from then on, I was terrified to get platelets. And I was to get them many more times.

The nurse said, "We'll have to see what her platelets are. They'll need to be up enough for surgery. They have to be over 80," which means 80,000. But my count was at just 14,000 before the platelets. Since I wasn't going to get more platelets that night, we wondered whether I could get the operation the next day. I felt relieved, sort of. But also a little freaked out. Without the operation, how could we start treatment?

Mom kept watch over me the whole night. We lay cuddled up together, and I slept a little. When Dad got home, he found the note and the cross I had left under the covers. He sent Mom a picture of the cross and the note. It made him cry. "How could she be thinking like this at seven years old? How can she be looking out for us when she's the one in need?"

He and Grant showed up at six the next morning. As they rode up the elevator, Grant turned to Dad. "Tell me the truth, Dad. Is Sadie going to die?"

Dad got choked up and hugged him. "No, Bud. She's going to be okay. We're going to get through this."

When they got to my room they sat on the couch, and we waited.

Finally, a nurse came in. She smiled. "Her platelets are up to 94," she said. Meaning 94,000.

We all looked at each other. Huh? How could my count go up by 80,000 in just a few hours? Maybe it was the ten minutes the platelets flowed into me. Maybe it was a miracle. This wouldn't be the last time we would think,

Miracle. There would be plenty more opportunities for miracles in the months to come.

At eight o'clock, a nurse transferred me onto a different bed and wheeled me into a big elevator. My family came with me, down to the first floor and then down long hallways where doctors and nurses were walking and sometimes running. I got pushed into a room with giant glass sliding doors. A nurse came in, hooked me up to fluids, and checked my vitals. An anesthesiologist had my parents sign a form. "You won't feel anything," he said, "and then you'll wake up."

The nurse came in with a gigantic syringe. She said, "This is a relaxer that will make you not remember anything." She pushed it into my IV so fast I could taste it, cold and metal, like I was a horse with a bit in my mouth. I yelped and then went blank. I thought I was asleep the whole time, but the drug they gave me, called Versed, actually keeps you awake but clueless and relaxed. I learned later that they asked me who was my favorite singer. "Katie Perry," I said. As they wheeled me out, a song came out loud from the nurse's phone, which she placed on my bed. It was Katie Perry's song "Roar."

I woke up, sort of, in a different room with a curtain hiding my bed from everything. I was crying. I felt sore in a spot right above my heart. That was where my port was. I felt it: a plasticky lump with tape over it. I knew there was a plastic tube in there. But at least I wouldn't get stuck with more needles. So there was that.

"How are you feeling?" There was a nurse beside my bed. She was checking a screen with my vitals and typing on a computer. "Would you like water or juice?"

"I'm good. Water, please." But I didn't feel good. I don't wake up well, especially from anesthesia. I'm not even a good nap taker. I feel like it's a waste of the day to take a nap. Four years later, I still freak out a little when I'm on a long car ride and start getting sleepy. It brings back memories of the 24 times I had to get anesthesia. Why would anyone take those sorts of drugs for fun?

Mom and Dad and Grant were in a waiting room. Dr. Engel called them into a consultation room. She said, "Sadie's doing well. Her port has been placed with no trouble, and this will help with all her chemo and blood transfusions. She won't need an IV anymore. While the surgeon was putting the port in, I went ahead and did the bone marrow biopsy, and she received her first dose of chemotherapy. I'll come by as soon as I get the results back."

Mom and Dad and Grant came in. I was fidgety and started crying. I wanted to yell, "Get me out of here!" But I didn't. I knew this was hard for them, too.

At noon, they took us back to the same room on the tenth floor. A nurse took the big, obnoxious IV out of my hand, and Mom and Dad got their first look at my port. It had a tube sticking out with a big butterfly clamp. This was going to be my new routine, but it would take some getting used to.

Dr. Engel came in with the result of the biopsy. "It's A-L-L, B-cell. She'll have two and a half years of chemotherapy with different phases to the therapies. But let's talk about what we're going to do now. She'll receive her next dose today." (If you wonder how I remember all this, it's because Mom wrote everything down and took pictures of everything, no matter how gross.)

The doctor turned to me. "Do you take pills?"

"No!" I had never taken a pill in my life. All the medicine until then had been liquid. I was a little kid. Little kids don't have to take pills, right?

"Trust me," Dr. Engel said. "You need to learn how to take pills." What she didn't tell me was, I was going to have to take as many as 20 or more pills a night.

She said I was going to be put on steroids as part of the treatment. "The taste of liquid steroids is the worst taste in the entire world," she said. "Child Life can come in and teach you how to take pills." She leaned in closer. "Sadie, even when I'm teaching the residents, I'll make them taste the dexamethasone so they know how bad it is." Dexamethasone is a powerful steroid, and they give it to you in high doses.

She gave Mom and Dad side effects sheets for all my chemo. "Here are the things she'll probably experience. Her hair could start falling out. Nausea is likely; we'll pretreat with Zofran to try to prevent that. She could experience jaw pain. Her legs could ache from the steroids." Dr. Engel was telling what to expect even before Mom and Dad read the sheets. "Her back may be sore from the bone-marrow biopsy."

As it turned out, those side effects sheets were like a prediction of the future.

Because of the itching episode, Dad and Grant decided to spend the next nights with us. Technically, Grant shouldn't have been allowed to stay. "We're staying together as a family," we said to each other. None of the nurses said anything about Grant staying. They just let him. It wasn't comfortable. Dad is a big guy. He turned part of our garage into a weight room, and he likes to lift weights after work. Grant was just ten back then, but he was a big ten. Today he's an offensive lineman on the football team, and he looked like a football player even back then.

We all slept so great that night...*not*. Dad and Grant were crammed into the little foldout couch. Mom and I slept in my twin-sized hospital bed. My back felt super sore. I started getting a pain in the back of my jaw on both sides, near my ears. The pain would cut all the way through my jaw for an hour at a time, and I started getting the most horrible migraines.

Still, for the next four days, I did a lot of crafts in my hospital room—gem art, bracelets, paint stuff, that sort of thing. I watched YouTube videos on my iPad, and watched TV with Grant. But one morning a migraine hit me, and I clenched in bed with a throbbing pain all around the top of my head. One night the headache got so bad I started gagging. I thought I was going to throw up, which made me freak out even more. The nurse gave me Tylenol and put some morphine in my port. But it took an hour for the medicine to help any. I had never had migraines in my life. We learned later that they were caused by high blood pressure. That's rare, a side effect of the steroid. The doctor put me on blood pressure medicine, and the migraines finally stopped. But the jaw pain continued. It would surprise me, like, *Hi, I'm your jaw pain! I'm back!* One minute I would be doing crafts, and another minute I was lying down crying in pain. Vincristine was the cause—one of the chemotherapy drugs.

Here's a weird fact: Scientists discovered vincristine in a pretty light-purple flower that grows on Texas ranches, called rose periwinkle. Another name for it is bright eyes.

Also, the graveyard plant.

Dr. Engel wanted to discharge me from the hospital on day four, but I was still having the headaches. Mom said she thought I should stay longer.

"That is totally fine," the doctor said. "You guys stay as long as you need."

We stayed another two days, and finally I felt better. We got a handle on my pain. Dr. Engel came in every day, the nurses were all really nice, and Caitlin, my child life specialist, brought me small candies—Nerds, M&Ms, that sort of thing—so I could practice swallowing pills. "Put the M&M on your tongue, then drink drink drink water." I practiced over and over and got it every time. Caitlin kept bringing me crafts kits from the toy closet. People donated them. And Jennifer, our social worker, helped our parents with paperwork and ways to deal with all the problems of having a kid with cancer. Jennifer is still our social worker, even today.

I got discharged late on a Tuesday night. It was about ten or 11. "There's a phone number you can call 24 hours a day," Dr. Engel told my parents. "If there's something going on that you're not sure about, call that number. That's why it's there. You can talk to the doctor on call and explain what's happening. They can guide you through it or have you come in." That gave Mom and Dad peace of mind. They could call anytime without feeling guilty.

When we got home, we saw a giant poster outside the garage:

WELCOME HOME SADIE

Our neighbors had made it. I thought, *I'm home!* It had seemed longer than a week since I had left. Every hour in that hospital had felt like a day.

Grant went inside, and when he opened the door my little dog Coco ran into the garage to greet me. I hugged and kissed her. Then I went straight up to my own room and went to bed. The whole family followed me, including Coco. She lay on my pillow and put her head on my forehead. It made me feel that she had been worried about me, too. Some dogs know whenever someone has cancer. They can sense it. It's special that my dog knew that something was wrong, and that she tried to comfort me.

The next day I just lay in bed all day and watched TV. The steroids made me tired and angry and upset. You can get super mad on steroids. It happens to most people. They call it *roid rage*. It can make kids angry at their own parents. But I don't like to be mean to my family, so I just cried. I felt so awful. My bones felt weak.

On Thursday I went to my first outpatient clinic, in the same hospital. Mom put Emla numbing cream (it's made of lidocaine) on my port and covered it with Press 'n Seal, a sticky kind of clear wrap. This was part of the instructions the nurse gave us.

A terrible ice storm hit just as we were heading out. We all piled into the car, and Dad drove on ice the whole way. It took us an hour and a half to get to the hospital. Even the weather seemed sick. I was wearing my big, hot pink puffy jacket and hugging my bear. Underneath I wore a long-sleeved black shirt with writing that said YOU GOT THIS GIRL! It became my slogan. It still is. You can find #yougotthisgirl on social media. In my room at home, I even have a picture frame with that hashtag on it.

At the hospital, we got taken back to a procedure waiting room. Caitlin was already there. She gave me an iPad to keep me distracted. The nurse cleaned my port with alcohol, which smelled really strong and wafted into my face. She took out a needle and asked me if I wanted to count to three.

"Yes."

She pushed it in, and I just felt some pressure. Then she took a Tegaderm sheet and stuck it on the port to keep it in place. She hooked me up to a fluid bag, and then I was taken into the procedure room. Dr. Engel came in and talked with us. I was trying to prepare myself, but I was super nervous. This would be my first time getting Propofol, which puts you to sleep but lets you wake up faster than with other drugs.

One of the nicest nurses, Christina, wheeled me a couple of rooms over. My parents came with me, while Grant stood waiting in the hallway. A bunch of people were already in the room: the anesthesiologist, a pair of medical students, Dr. Engel, and some nurses. I was trembling. The lights were glaring bright, and they glittered off big machines. I had no idea what those things were. The anesthesiologist took out a humongous tube filled with thick white liquid: the Propofol. I couldn't believe all that was going into my body. He picked up the tube that came out of my port and put the syringe into it, pushing very slowly—I had asked him not to go fast. I felt this cold, cold liquid in my throat. It moved through my body into my veins, chilling me all over. I could taste it—growing in my throat, like the most bitter pill that someone crushed up with a drop of water and shoved down me. Some people say it tastes like metal, but not me. It tastes like...like alcohol and bitterness. I saw black spots, like what you see when you rub your eyes when you're tired— black splotches. My eyes began closing, and I felt I was floating in the air. Some of my friends say they love that Propofol feeling. They say it's like flying. I think it's creepy. It's like suddenly leaving your body and levitating off the bed.

And then the noises around me became silence and I woke up in a totally different room with different people in it, plus my family.

"Do you want any water?" a nurse asked me.

I did. I still had a weird taste in my mouth, and I was thirsty and hungry. They don't let you eat or drink anything all night before a procedure. So the nurse held out a basket of snacks—chips, animal crackers, Granola bars—and I picked mini pretzels. She then gave me a Styrofoam cup with a tiny straw, and I sipped some water. After a spinal tap, water tastes like Propofol. The water actually strengthens the chemical taste. You want to drink, but it's awful. I ate a lot of pretzels to get that Propofol taste out of my mouth.

Before I even woke up, Caitlin had shown up with Dr. Engel and led Grant off to another room for some snacks. We learned later that whenever Child Life came with Dr. Engel, it meant a private conversation and not great news. Dr. Engel took my parents aside. She was holding the lab work. "Sadie did great," she said. "We administered methotrexate in her spine. But she still has 8.5 percent leukemia cells in her blood. We really want one percent."

Mom and Dad just looked at her. So was this bad?

"I'm still confident we can get this," Dr. Engel said. "But we need to keep an eye on it. This just means we can't label her low risk."

So...?

She explained that leukemia works differently from other kinds of cancer. With other cancers, doctors talk about stages, like one to four, usually using Roman numerals for some reason: *I* to *IV*. With leukemia, doctors talk instead about the risk of the cancer coming back. "Sadie was diagnosed early," Dr. Engel said. "And because of her white blood cell count at the time of diagnosis"—it wasn't that terribly low or that horribly high—"we know Sadie probably won't be very high risk."

Which was...good news?

"But," she said. "Based on what we saw today, we know she can't be low risk."

So now what?

"What it will come down to is what we'll learn on Day 29, with the next bone marrow biopsy," she said. This meant that 29 days after diagnosis, they would do another spinal tap. (*Fun!*) If they found zero percent cancer cells, then I would be "standard" risk. If they found any cancer cells at all, I would be high risk.

How about no risk? That wasn't in the picture. And... risk of what? Nobody was talking to me about that.

CHAPTER FOUR

When You Want a Puppy, They Have to Give You One

We went home, and I lay on the couch and slept a lot. That night, though, when I was about to take a bath, I looked in the mirror. My left shoulder was hunched up much higher than my right one. I came into my parents' bedroom and shouted, "I can't put my shoulder down!"

Mom pushed down on it and it wouldn't move. "Try lifting your arm above your head."

I couldn't. It was stiff. That was freaky.

Mom called the number Dr. Engel gave me. The on-call doctor called back and said, "Maybe she's just uncomfortable because she was accessed for the first time." He meant that the chemo had been put through my port, and maybe my body wasn't used to it. "Keep an eye on it, and if anything changes call again," the doctor said.

I took a bath and slept in my parents' bed and forgot about it.

The next morning I woke up with a terrible pain in my jaw, and I felt achy all over. Before Mom got me pain medicine, she took my temperature with one of those head scanners. The medicine, morphine, can disguise a fever. Dr. Engel had told Mom that if my temperature was 100.5 degrees or higher, she should take me right back to the hospital. The thermometer read 99.9.

Right then Dr. Engel called. She said laboratory results to see how the leukemia grows showed I wasn't at any higher risk. "This is good news," she said. "I wanted to let you know."

"Great!" Mom said. "While I have you..." and she told about my temperature.

"Take it again in 30 minutes, and if it goes up to 100.5, give me a call and come in again."

Mom, being Mom, took it again right away: 101.5. She started packing. I was really upset, because I knew we had to go back to the hospital. She called Dad, who left his job after just an hour and a half of being back at work. And we picked up Grant from school. The three of us drove to Children's, hoping we wouldn't be admitted.

Dr. Engel and one of the nurses were waiting at the door to our room. Caitlin came and had me play Candy Crush while the nurse was accessing my port, putting in an antibiotic, Rocephin. They drew labs out of my port that day and grew the bacteria in my blood to see if there was an infection. My ANC, the immune system number, was just about zero. If it's under 500 and you're in an emergency room, you get admitted. The rule is, in the first 29 days if you get fever you stay in until day 29. So at that point we knew we were going to be in the hospital for the rest of the month.

They took us into a room on the sixth floor. We had been home for only a day and a half. Later that day the doctor said I had sepsis, an infection of my blood—meaning I had two bad things, cancer and the bacteria, in one. Actually, the bacteria they found, E. coli, is in everyone's body. But because of my chemo and my non-working immune system, I couldn't keep that bacteria in check.

The area all around my port turned bright red, and over the next ten days my room was a revolving door. Every single day, all day, all night, there was somebody in my room besides my family. I would wake up with ten doctors and nurses, infectious disease people, social workers, physical therapists to see if I could move my shoulder. An orthopedic surgeon came to see if the infection was going into my bone. Almost every one of them checked my heartbeat. I got MRI and CT scans, sonograms, X-rays, lab work, physical therapy. I got depressed and angry, and I cried and didn't leave my room. I didn't want to talk to anybody. I was just over it.

"I'm just sick of this. I wish it would all go away," I said to Mom. While the doctors and nurses were still in the room, I took my notebook and a black Crayola marker and wrote "NO NURSES ALLOWED." I handed it to Mom.

Then Dr. Engel put up a sign. It said doctors and nurses were not allowed in during Sadie's Time, an hour or two a day, unless there was an emergency. And she scheduled Cluster Care, when all the doctors watching me—including two infectious disease doctors, the social worker, nurses, and others—would come all at the same time. That way I could get some rest and not get poked and measured all the time.

After the MRIs, we found out that the infection was spreading to my port. Which meant I had to get surgery again to remove the port, and the wound would have to be kept open to let it drain, healing from the inside out, over two or three months. Meanwhile I'd get a PICC line, putting medicine into my arm. Three months later I ended up getting a port in my right side.

To this day, I look like I was shot in the shoulder on my left side, where the original port was and where it got infected. I like my scar. It's super cool.

So during that stretch in the hospital, I went under general anesthesia five times. Five times to get wheeled onto the elevator, away from Mom and Dad. Five times to get knocked out. Five times waking up thirsty and hungry with a horrible taste in my mouth. It went like this:

> **First surgery:** Getting my port put in.
> **Second:** Taking it out, because my blood
>   got infected.
> **Third:** PICC line in. (A catheter instead
>   of the port.)
> **Fourth:** PICC line out, after the wound
>   finally healed.
> **Fifth:** Port in, this time on the other side.

Halfway through my stay, Dad said, "It feels like we've been here for three months." I didn't hear the "It feels like." I thought he said, "We've been here for three months." So when people in the hospital asked how long I'd been in, I'd say: "I've been here three months!" And at that point it had been just two weeks. And I had to stay another two weeks after that. That's what a hospital stay does: It messes with time.

They were keeping me in for my blood counts, waiting for my ANC, the measurement of my immune system,

41

to come back up. If I went home, I might risk another infection. And the infection I already had needed to be 100 percent cleared.

Around that time, even though the steroids made me hungry, I wouldn't eat the hospital food.

"What do you want?" Mom said. "We can order your meal."

"I don't want any of that. I just want your rice or your noodles or pork chops."

So Dad cooked up scrambled eggs with bits of sausage in them the next morning, and he brought it in a baggie. From then on, he and Mom brought food in bulk, putting it in a fridge reserved for parents. It was great. I'd say, "I want cheese biscuits," and they would bring cheese biscuits. There are pictures Mom took of me eating in my hospital bed. On the tray are five Styrofoam bowls of buttered noodles, mashed potatoes with butter, buttered white rice, ribs a neighbor cooked, and curly fries. The fries were the only thing from the hospital I would eat. Which I did just about every day.

In other words, pretty much the only things I ate were white stuff and meat and curly fries. So healthy! It's hard to say anything great about having cancer, but here's one thing: When people are worried about you dying, they don't fuss with you much.

Besides making me hungry, the steroids swelled me up in places. I was taking them twice a day that whole first month, and then again during a couple phases later. The steroids help kill the cancer. But almost all cancer kids get a moon face. I had huge cheeks and a pot belly—another side effect. In the mirror, I looked like somebody else. That wasn't Sadie; it was some very weird chipmunk kid.

Gradually, though, I started to perk up. Mom and Dad talked me into walking the halls as much as five times a day. "Come on," they would say. "You'll feel so much better after you do." And they were right. Walking was especially helpful after I ate. Because of the steroids making me hungry all the time, I stuffed myself, which made me feel miserable. At home, before I got cancer, we would walk around the block after meals to get my stomach moving. So we did the same thing in the hospital: I put on my hot pink robe and we walked in a loop from my room down the hall, around the admissions section and back, while Mom pushed my IV pole. The nurses called me The Girl Who Walks.

I didn't know it at the time, but this was our big answer to cancer. The doctors and nurses did what they could. But the thing that was up to me was: *get moving*. The walking would be just the beginning.

We were walking down a hall at one point when a nurse was passing by. She stopped. "Sarah?"

Mom said, "Yes?"

"I'm Brittany," the nurse said. "I used to work at Anthropologie with you." Mom was the district manager, and Brittany worked at one of the stores. "Why are you here?" Brittany asked.

She took me under her wing and was so special to me. She's a fun person, and all the kids' favorite nurse. She plays Barbie with the girls and Nerf gun battles with the boys. And she does this while taking care of her patients, doing chemo and labs, and typing on her computer.

One day, Brittany came into my room. "Sadie!" she said. "You're not wearing green!"

"Why?"

"It's Saint Patrick's Day!"

"It is?" We had lost track of time.

"You don't want to get pinched. Put these on." She gave me a headband with green pom poms on top, and she put a green beaded necklace around my neck. She stood back and admired me. "There. Now you won't get pinched." By a leprechaun, she meant. She knew how to make me smile.

Another favorite nurse was Kelly. She could tell exactly what I was going through, like she was reading my mind. This was understandable—Kelly had gone through cancer herself when she was a child. She knew that saying the right things, being positive, telling a kid what was going to happen before every poke and prod, were important. And that toys could do as much to make a child feel better as pain medicine does. Or even more. I loved Kelly. All the kids loved her, and she loved us.

Dr. Engel also knew what to do to cheer me up. She said to me, "When you're a childhood cancer patient, people always ask what you want. Don't pass up that opportunity. Tell them what you want."

I told my parents I wanted my dog, Coco. Mom named her after Coco Chanel, the famous fashion designer.

There are pet therapy dogs in the hospital, and some volunteers bring their dogs. "Can you bring Coco up here?" I asked my parents.

"Oh, I don't think that's such a good idea," Mom said. "The nurses probably wouldn't like Coco up here."

I knew she was right. Coco is a queen. She likes to be in charge and do her own thing. When she's not sleeping, a lot of the time she likes to be left alone. Mom reminded me that Coco could snap at one of the other kids.

What I really wanted was a puppy, a tiny adorable puppy. I told Dr. Engel.

She said, "Say you want a puppy, and then they have to give it to you." Which was kind of a joke, but really not. "Just give her a puppy," she said to Mom and Dad.

"Y'all are ganging up on me!" Dad said.

And then my hair began to fall out. It happens to most kids with cancer, only it's not the cancer. It's the treatment, the medicine, the good poison that kills the cancer also but makes you lose your hair. Plus your eyebrows and even your eyelashes.

When I first learned my hair would probably fall out, I freaked out. I'm a girl. I like having hair. And the thought of going to school as a bald girl just didn't seem bearable. Mom talked about our options: a wig, scarves, hats... I said I wanted a wig. But what I wanted was my own hair, forever. When I'm nervous, I twirl my hair through my fingers. After being on treatment for a while, when I twirled my hair it came out on my fingers. Then it fell in chunks, leaving just strands of hair. I started touching

45

Mom's hair when I was with her. One day, when I was with my friend Makayla, I found myself holding her hair and softly feeling it. It made me think, *This is what being a girl feels like.*

But our doctor said that for most kids with cancer, their hair grows back over the rest of the treatment and doesn't fall out again. This gave me hope. And sure enough, one day I looked in the mirror and saw...eyelashes and eyebrows! Very faint, but still. Hair.

"Mom!" I ran to her. "Look at this!"

And then it fell out again. And again. And again. The wind would blow my hair right out. The problem was vincristine, the cancer drug I was on. The poison. Going bald just once, that was supposed to be it. But I had to be different.

Mom has a good friend, Miss Cassie, who's a hairstylist. She came to cut my hair in a bob. My hair was already starting to fall out from the chemo, and it was matting in the back where my head lay against the pillow. I didn't feel like brushing it. Cassie knew I had wanted for years to dye my hair a fun color, and my parents had always said no. "Well," Cassie said to Mom, "her hair is going to fall out anyway. Why not color it?"

She pulled up a chair in front of the bed. I sat in it, and she cut my hair into a bob. Then she took out pink dye and started slapping it on my hair. When I saw myself in the mirror, I had the biggest smile. I saw a new girl with shorter hair and streaks of bright pink. It was the change I had wanted for a long time. My cousins were there, and they took pictures and admired me. I walked the halls after that and The Girl Who Walks became The Girl with Pink Hair Who Walks.

The pink stayed until all my hair fell out six months after diagnosis. I waited a really long time to shave my head. There were just strands of pink, patches of bald, and regular hair, all over my head. It looked awful. It made me look even sicker than I was.

One night when I was home, I made a video with my mom in her closet. I wanted to cut off all the extra strands. Before the video, I took a small mirror and scissors into the closet and cut my hair. Mom helped with the back. It was just fuzz, but I looked healthier. I explained on the video, "Hair doesn't really matter. What matters is on the inside." It's one of the biggest videos I did. (I'll tell you about the videos later. They led to a lot of amazing things for me.)

I don't really need hair to be myself. I was still the same Sadie on the inside. I ended up not wearing a wig. Still, I wish I had pink hair today. It'd be fun to look different. Mom and Dad say, "Uh-uh."

After three weeks in the hospital, during the weekend, a doctor came into my room. We hadn't seen her before. The oncologists take turns on weekends. "You're looking really good," she said. "You're probably going home on Monday."

I was so excited and ready.

"Really?" Mom said. Dr. Engel had said I would have to stay at least another week.

"Yeah, I think it's time."

On Monday, the nurse said, "We're going to let you go home." She had the instructions from the weekend doctor.

"Let's go!" I yelled. "I can't wait to get home."

But we had to wait for all the paperwork, which takes forever. Dad packed all our things up and brought it to the car, and then we sat around, just waiting.

Another oncologist came in. He said, "We talked to Dr. Engel, and we really don't want to send you guys home until everything is, without a doubt, all clear. We're going to need to keep you another week."

I wasn't paying attention.

Mom put a hand on my shoulder. "Did you hear what he said?"

"No, what?"

"Baby, they want to make sure you're all good. So we have to stay another week.

"You're kidding, right? That's a joke?" I really thought she was kidding.

"No, Honey. We don't want to have to come back. I'm so sorry."

I'm usually a slow crier—just a few tears with no sound is my way of crying. But this time I bawled really loud. My mind went ballistic. I was still on steroids, which make you like the Incredible Hulk inside. It had been three weeks of steroids and frustration.

"How could they do that?" I screamed. "How could they say I was going home and then not let me? They're all liars. Everyone here is a liar!" It seemed like people had been lying to me the whole time. They told me I was going home, and then I was stuck in the hospital. It was like they were doing this on purpose.

I now know that all that was just part of dealing with a complicated disease. Those people weren't lying to me. They were just being hopeful. I had the best care from brilliant experts. But sometimes the signals just got crossed.

Which, when you think about it, is a little like cancer itself. Leukemia isn't some evil monster who's out to kill you. It's just a cell. One that crosses its signals. It forgets part of its code.

"Reproduce yourself," the code says.

"Okay," the cell says.

"Then die."

"What?"

And it keeps reproducing itself, forgetting the code that says it's supposed to die. And those cells it makes never know that part of the code in the first place, and they reproduce not knowing to die. Those cells are just part of you. They're not the enemy. They're just a part of you that got their signals crossed.

Those same cells, the leukemia, taught me to be a fighter. I was fighting the cancer, the pain, the frustration of being stuck in the hospital. I was fighting the fear. But the weird thing was, I was fighting what was inside me. Not some alien germ or whatever. It was a part of me. When I got chemo, it was like, *No hard feelings, okay? It's just that you're supposed to die.*

49

I *wasn't* supposed to die.

Dad went and unloaded the car. Nobody could believe this. The hospital stay had been hard enough. It was like everybody was being wonderful while doing the opposite at the same time. The nurses and doctors and my parents were my best friends, but they were the same ones putting my port in and sticking needles in me and telling me I couldn't leave.

Think about it. What if you said, "My friend stuck a needle in me." Wouldn't that be confusing? Or make you think maybe that wasn't such a good friend?

I wrote on the window of my hospital room, DON'T BUG ME and NO POKE ZONE. At the same time, I knew all those pokes and prods were supposed to save my life. But why were they telling me one thing that would get my hopes up and then telling me the opposite? How could I trust these people? I wouldn't stop crying.

Mom knew what to do. She texted my babysitter, Miss Alex. I love Miss Alex. She's my best friend even though she's older. She had just graduated from college and was waiting to go to occupational therapy school. On the very first day that Miss Alex babysat Grant and me, she didn't use her phone the whole time. Instead she did whatever Grant and I wanted to do. She lives in Fort Worth now, about 30 miles away, so I don't get to see her as often. But when I do, we go rock climbing at an indoor climbing gym. It's a tradition. And we also go to a trampoline park called Altitude.

"Can I come see her?" Alex said.

"That would be the best thing ever!" Mom said.

Miss Alex came two hours later. It was a total surprise. Mom hadn't told me she was coming. I had the biggest smile on my face. She brought me a memory game that was based on *Adventure Time,* a TV show I love. Mom joined us in playing that game, and Miss Alex stayed until nine or ten at night. For part of that, we sat together and just talked. It was like the least bitter kind of medicine.

And then, for the next week, my family and I were in a holding pattern. Every morning at four o'clock, a nurse would come in and draw labs, taking blood from my PICC line. Mom would go out afterward to the nurses' station to ask to see the lab work. She had learned to read it like a doctor. She was hoping to see a good blood count so I could go home.

One of those days, Mom saw that there was a new nurse assigned to us. She said that an oncologist on service that week seeing the inpatient kids had asked Mom to wait before letting her see the lab work. "Let me page him and have him come to your room," the nurse said.

He came in shortly after and explained to us about what they call "blasts," cells that show up that aren't normal. The word is a nickname for myeloblasts, which are immature blood cells. Blasts can be cancer cells. When I was first diagnosed, they saw 25,000 of them. "Sometimes because of the chemo, blasts can show up and not be cancer cells," the doctor said.

It was another moment of panic.

This was like going on a blind roller coaster ride that seems to last forever. The seatbelt won't come undone, and you can't get off. You go side to side, and then you're going up so high, and the next second you're dropping so fast your stomach can't catch up. What I couldn't see at the time was that, after a year, things would start to get a little better. The roller coaster would straighten out and take me on a great journey.

But I wasn't thinking about any of that at the time. We were just trying to get through the day. Sometimes it was a struggle just to get through the hour, or the moment. To get through the pain.

Before we went to sleep, I would say a prayer that the next day would be a better one without side effects:

Dear Lord, please make tomorrow a better day than today. Please make me sleep super good and make me feel energized tomorrow. Please look after me while I'm getting my chemo. Cure my cancer, and thank you for everything, amen.

Sometimes I would pray for other people, like if a friend was having a hard time with their cancer or anything else. I prayed to help the doctors, especially Dr. Engel. I prayed for her to help the other kids and me. The weird thing is, when you pray to please make other people feel better, it makes you feel better. The effort comes with a built-in reward.

Before I got diagnosed, we weren't regular church people. We skipped a lot of Sundays. Now we go every week, and we're much more active. In our church, they do a lot of kid stuff and conferences, and I find them really inspiring. It was as if we all needed the nudge.

A couple days after the doctor told us about the blasts, they turned out to be a false alarm. And finally, we got to go home. As soon as they saw us, neighbors started cooking. Dinner that first time was roast beef with carrots and green beans, cooked in a crockpot by a neighbor. It was so good to eat a homecooked meal. Dad loved it; it was his kind of meal.

I ate just the meat. I'm a meat girl.

A week later, I got another bone marrow biopsy with the spinal tap and chemo and the nasty Propofol. That was Day 29, the big day for seeing whether there was any cancer left in me. But we wouldn't know until the results came back a few days later.

This was a big deal. If no cancer cells showed up, I would be Standard Risk. If they found cancer still in me, then I would be High Risk. Which would mean I would have to go back to the hospital. It would also mean getting a big bag of methotrexate, which pretty much wipes out your blood count along with the cancer, and you have to get lots of blood transfusions, and the doctors have to watch you all the time to make sure you don't get infected. And the big problem was, I was already infected. My wound hadn't healed yet. Even when I got out of the hospital, I had to go back twice a week to have my wound packed, and I had to get antibiotics through my PICC line every day. Mom learned how to do it at home.

Mom and Dad were going crazy. Me, I was just so glad to go home.

CHAPTER FIVE

It's Easier to Talk in a Closet Than on the Ellen Show

A couple days after I got home, we had to go back to the clinic to get my wound cleaned and packed. The first time they did that in the hospital, I was distracted and it didn't hurt much. This time at the clinic, I was super scared. A wound care specialist came in with a packet—gauze, tape, a lot of packing. It looked like a thin ribbon of felt. I was crying because I thought it was going to hurt. But then, I had no choice.

That's one of the things about getting medical care: You don't usually get what you want. When it comes to cancer, it's like, *Do you want to live or not?* So the choice isn't about chemo or wound care. It's whether you're going to get through it in the best way possible and come out the other end.

I mean, it's like this: Your life says to you, *You have cancer. Deal with it.* So your choice becomes how you deal with it. Which is the hardest kind of choice, especially for a kid. We get fewer choices than adults do. That's why I think it's important to make sure that, whenever possible, we should give kids good kinds of choices. Like what kind of toy you want, or what you want for dessert. The easier choices make us stronger for the harder choices.

They took off my bandage while I was lying down on the hospital bed. Mom was there, looking closely. I wasn't. They had said, "It's going to open up and start healing." In the beginning it had been a wide slit. A few days later, here in the hospital room, it was now an inch-deep hole the size of a half dollar. Mom had to act like it was no big deal. She wanted to gasp and say, "Is this normal?" Instead she had to hold my hand while trying to hold it together and while I was crying. She stayed strong. I couldn't read her emotions.

But then my tests came back. It was Day 29 after my diagnosis, and Mom and Dad seemed like they were holding their breath that entire time. The doctor drew my bone marrow again, and sent it to the lab again. Back it came: The leukemia was gone. I was in remission! I could be put into the Standard Risk protocol, meaning the chance of cancer coming back was lower than in Higher Risk. I still faced a couple of years of chemo, but we could celebrate.

We could celebrate, but even then we knew we had a long ways to go. Back when I got diagnosed, Dad asked Dr. Engel, "When's the party?" He meant, *When do we celebrate the end of chemo?* Dr. Engel said she couldn't say yet. For weeks and weeks after that, she and other doctors and nurses kept handing Mom sheets explaining the drugs and their side effects. I got chemo thousands of times—infusions in my port, through my PICC line, into my spine, and from pills.

None of the medicines were new. Almost all of them were older than my parents. One of the most important cancer drugs I took was vincristine. People had been using it for all kinds of cures hundreds of years ago. Doctors started treating cancer patients with it in 1963. Seriously. Half a century ago. It's still one of the most important cancer drugs. Up until 2019, only two drug companies in the whole world made vincristine. Then one of those companies decided not to make it any more, leaving just one company to make it. As we were finishing this book, there was a shortage of the drug. Parents of cancer kids were praying they could get it, even though they knew that vincristine can cause all kinds of side effects for the rest of a kid's life. Including my life. The doctors keep talking about my heart even though it's been a couple years since I took vincristine, because the drug can damage your heart.

Another cancer drug I took was doxorubicin. Called the Red Devil because it's colored red, you can watch it creep toward you through the tube into your port. It makes most kids really sick, and they throw up again and again. But I was lucky. I never once got sick from it.

I also got a drug called 6MP every night for a year and a half. The full name is mercaptopurine, and it made me lose weight, go really pale, and feel tired all the time. Also: dexamethasone, the steroid that caused my face to puff up and made me feel really angry and sad and hungry. Also: cyclophosphamide, which causes you to lose your hair and can make wounds hard to heal.

At the same time, all the attention and support I got made me think. Were other cancer kids getting everything I was getting? Do all the kids get block parties and love? Did they have doctors who explained everything? I wanted to do something for the other kids. But I had just turned eight years old. What could I possibly do?

One night, around eight or nine, I was sitting around super bored. Which gave me an idea. Before cancer, whenever I was bored, I liked to go into Mom's closet and make a video with her phone while I went through her clothes. Mom worked at Kate Spade back then as a district manager, which meant she got lots of great dresses and shoes. I did a YouTube series called *Sadie's Fashion.*

This time, I took my iPad and all my medical stuff: my wound care, PICC line, antibiotics, saline syringe, gauze and tape and packing stuff—plus Heparin, a drug that keeps your blood from clotting and clogging up the PICC line. It took several trips to bring all that stuff through my parents' bedroom into the closet. Mom was lying on the bed, watching TV.

"Whatever you do," I said, "don't come in. I'm making a video."

I sat on the floor with all the medical things, hit the video button, and said, "Hello, I'm Sadie Keller, and I'm..."

"What are you doing?" It was Grant. He had walked right in when he heard my voice.

"Leave! I'm making a video!"

He left, and I began again.

"I'm Sadie Keller, and I'm going to tell you all about what happens when you have cancer." I talked for 17 minutes and 32 seconds, going through every piece of equipment, showing my port, and telling why I was bald. I explained everything about having ALL B-cell leukemia. I talked about what a port is and how it lets all the medicine get into your body. "Some people, when they first get cancer, they're really nervous about it. And I'm just going to talk to you guys about it and make it feel easier than what it usually seems like to you."

I told how when you get an operation and are put to sleep, you don't feel anything, even though it seems scary beforehand. I talked about all the things that the doctors and nurses were going to do to me in the weeks ahead. I showed the PICC line and the flush and the Heparin and how they worked. I showed how you can cut a sock in half to cover your PICC line. In the video, I look like it's all a natural thing, like I'm explaining math or toenail art.

The video explained what it's like to have cancer. I talked about the nice people you meet in the hospital. "After a couple of months of having it, you're pretty calm because you're actually feeling better. And when you actually get to go home, it's like the best day of your life." I told how you feel pretty tired then.

Whenever I talked about the bad things, like being on steroids and having to go back to the hospital, I then told all the good things, like the movies you get to watch in the hospital and the dogs that Child Life and some nurses bring, along with the toys you might get because so many people care you have cancer. Finally, I showed the printouts of counts that tell how your blood is doing. And I ended with this: "If you ever had cancer, I hope that this video really made you feel good. And if you still have cancer, I hope it made you feel not so scared anymore." Now, five years later, I don't know how I managed to talk like that. I was just seven years old.

I called the video *Sadie's Journey.*

I came out with my iPad. Mom and Dad were in the bedroom. "I need you guys to watch this."

When it was over, Mom said, "I didn't know you were paying attention all that time!" Mom and Dad thought I never listened when Dr. Engel was talking about my cancer and the treatments. I was usually on my iPad the whole time, and it looked like I was ignoring them. But really I was listening. I was learning a lot. Now they knew.

I asked Mom to post it on YouTube, and it got thousands of views. Here's what I didn't know: Those 17 minutes were just the beginning of my speaking in front of people. Millions of people.

At the end of August, I was supposed to start third grade. Instead, I was admitted into the hospital with a fever. I had no ANC—no immune system. I stayed a week. I was going to do homebound school; I wouldn't have gone to the regular school anyway, because of the risk of infection from other kids. But still. First day of school. While other kids were posting their first-day photos, I was stuck in the hospital. I went into the playroom and made a poster: FIRST DAY OF THIRD GRADE. I stood out in the hallway and took a picture. You can see in the photo that my left eye was swollen. That morning I had gotten a lot of fluids and then slept on my left side. The swelling lasted the whole day.

It wasn't long after that when I experienced what looked like a stroke, when I couldn't talk. This was one of more than 35 times we had to rush to the emergency room or the clinic. We often didn't get home until the early hours of the morning, sometimes not at all. This time it was two in the morning, and I hadn't eaten since lunch. I was starving. The steroid that helps fights the cancer makes you feel really, really hungry. I lay in the hospital bed and dozed off while Dad went to get something for us to eat. He got in the car and went to a Taco Cabana for breakfast tacos. I ate some and went to sleep.

I felt much better the next morning. Back to normal. The on-call oncologist came in with four students. It's a teaching moment whenever I'm around because I get so many weird side effects. The doctor explained that I had methotrexate neurotoxicity, a swelling of brain cells caused by the chemo. Ten days earlier, I had received a methotrexate spinal tap. That's what caused my symptoms, because the medicine goes up the spinal fluid. It took its time traveling up, then messed with my cells. The swelling caused the brain waves not to get through right. The signals wouldn't go through to my arm. My brain would go, *What? I told you to pick up that chicken nugget!* But it was like the wifi on the channel to my arm went down.

He then explained the leucovorin, and said that Dr. Engel would get an action plan. I was supposed to get another spinal tap in a couple weeks. (*Oh, boy!*) Then the neurologist came in and asked Mom and Dad to step into the hallway. That's never a good sign.

"Now what are we supposed to do?" Mom asked. "She's supposed to get a spinal tap with methotrexate again in a couple of weeks."

"If it was my child, I wouldn't let her have any more methotrexate," the doctor said.

What?

They discharged us, and when we got home, Mom and Dad requested a meeting with Dr. Engel. She already had a game plan in place. When they met, she walked Mom and Dad through it. "It's a very important part of the treatment plan for Sadie," she said. She explained, "This can happen, though it's very rare. The good news is, it almost never happens twice. It's an isolated event. The methotrexate thins the folate around the cell, and the leucovorin puts folate back in. We don't want to continue that with every procedure if we don't have to, because of the chance that it might counteract the effects of the medicine."

This all made me even more nervous about the procedures. Every time, Dr. Engel would give Mom and Dad a list of the side effects on everything. They'd be in columns for Rare, Normal, and Common. But I was getting side effects not even listed on the page. It's partly why all the medical students loved me. I had all these interesting side effects. (Plus, soon after this episode, I started bringing them cupcakes.)

Then a producer for *The Ellen DeGeneres Show* called Mom's phone. We were cooking dinner. "Hi, Sarah, this is Jocylyn from *Ellen!*"

"Sadie! Get down here, it's the *Ellen* show!"

I love Ellen. I watched her show throughout treatment. I'm a huge fan. I love how she's funny and pulls pranks on everyone and plays games with the audience members. She has a kind heart, and she donates money to lots of causes.

I ran downstairs. Was someone playing a prank on us?

Mom put the call on speaker. "We saw Sadie's story," Jocylyn said. Meaning my closet video. "We'd love to talk to her." She said they were really proud of what we were doing and would love to Skype with me. So they set up a video Skype for the following week. The next week, I sat with Mom's phone in her office, sitting at her black desk. I was really shy, and I wasn't talking much. I was alone.

The producer started by making chitchat. "Did you know that Ellen was the voice of Dory in *Finding Nemo?*"

"Um, noooo. She is?"

"Yes!"

"That's, uh, really awesome."

"Okay, Sadie, so I'm going to go off the screen. When I come back, pretend I'm Ellen."

I thought maybe it would actually *be* Ellen. Otherwise, why would she leave the screen? But when she came back it was still the same producer.

I'm not a really good actor. "Oh...my..gosh..you're amazing," I said. Like I was reading a boring story. I had no idea what to say.

The producer asked to put my mom on. "Have you guys been approached by any other shows?"

"No," Mom said. "Just local television."

"If you would just not tell anyone we've reached out to you. If you're approached by any other shows, please let us know before talking to them."

And we thought, *Could other shows get in touch?*

I told Dr. Engel, "I'm not supposed to tell you this, but the *Ellen* show called."

"Sadie! Ellen always gives you something. This is your chance to get a puppy!" Dr. Engel was always working the puppy angle. I just love that doctor.

A week later, the producer emailed Mom: "We love Sadie so much! You can talk to other shows now." Which was a polite way of saying I wouldn't be on the *Ellen* show.

It turned out this was an audition, though nobody had told me that. This was my big chance to tell everybody about childhood cancer and maybe get her to give me a puppy. And I blew it.

CHAPTER SIX

The Toy Blizzard

This wasn't the best time for me. We had to go to clinic two times a week. Once a week I got the whole deal: chemo, wound care, and a cleaning of my PICC line. This lasted for months, which when you're eight years old is basically forever, especially when you're just starting treatment and see clinic after clinic in your future. I didn't want to go to the first clinic. That morning I kind of freaked out even before I got in the car.

But when we got there, I saw Flick, one of my cancer friends, giving out cupcakes to the doctors and nurses. His Mom, Kcee, is a really good baker. (The other kids in the family are Banjo and Jubilee.) All the medical people looked excited to get the treats, and I thought, *That's a really cool idea!* While sitting in the clinic, I looked for ideas on Pinterest, using an iPad. This was in early April, a couple weeks before Easter, so I searched "Easter treats." Up popped a picture of a rabbit made out of a Styrofoam cup, with paper ears, googly eyes, and paper circles for cheeks.

Mom and I bought plastic wrappers at a baking store, stuffed one of them into a cup, and then filled the cup with candy. We made a bunch of those. I cut out every single circle and ear myself. And it changed everything. I couldn't wait to go back to clinic so I could give Dr. Engel and all my nurses, including Brittany, the treats.

The next week I got little jars the size of medicine bottles and filled them with jelly beans. I wrote labels for each one:

CHILL PILLS. TAKE TWO PILLS DAILY
WHEN STRESSED. IF NO PROGRESS,
FIND SADIE IMMEDIATELY.

I made 20 of those, buying the bottles at Hobby Lobby. Every week after that I made something different. After clinic I would say, "What are we going to make next?" The nurses couldn't wait to see what I would come up with. So I got into baking. I made cupcakes, and sugar cookies with NO MORE CANCER on them, and a circle with CANCER and a line through it. And I wrote other stuff like #1 BEST DOCTOR EVER. I put the cookies in little wooden boxes from Hobby Lobby and painted the boxes with a marker. I put a name on each one: Dr. Engel, Jennifer our social worker, Caitlin the child life specialist, Fatima the blood woman, and nurses Brittany, Maria, Jen, Kelly, Christina, and Lane, and a bunch more.

Mom and I went to the dollar store and stocked up on candy. We got see-through cups colored orange and green. Orange is the color for leukemia, just as pink is the color for breast cancer. And green was my favorite color. (It's blue now. Kids change.) The cups were like tumblers with a straw. We bought Snickers, Hershey's, and other candy, and I put people's names on the cups with a little label.

At Christmas, we made candy sleighs. You take a big KitKat bar and two candy canes, and use hot glue to stick them on the candy bar. That's the sleigh. Then you take little square chocolates still in their wrappers and glue them in a pile like a stack of presents. And you tie the whole thing with a gold or red ribbon.

This giving went on all year.

The day after I got home from my neurotoxicity episode at the hospital, Mom drove me to Miss Kcee's house— Flick's mom. She had invited me to come bake with her. The plans had been made before I got neurotoxicity. "We have to go," I told Mom. "There's no way we're not going."

Miss Kcee asked me what kind of cake I wanted to make. She showed me all her cake pans. She had a lot of them. I picked the biggest one. "I want three tiers," I said. "Like a wedding cake."

"All right, we can do that," she said.

So, one day my arm doesn't work and I can't talk. The next day I'm baking a humongous cake. I took it to my nurses, and they loved it.

My friends started giving me baking stuff when they found out I love to bake. I go through phases. This was my baking phase. It went on for a year, and we have a full cart of baking tools—cookie cutters, piping bags. I baked as much as three times a day, giving a lot of it to our neighbors.

September was my first Childhood Cancer Awareness Month. The night before, I said, "We should do a bake sale."

"Okay," Mom said. "I'll post it on the Lantana page." That's a Facebook page for our neighborhood.

So the next morning, I woke up and yelled, "I'm baking!" This was heaven for me. I made sugar cookies with icing. While those were baking, I made cupcakes, and while those were baking, I iced the cookies. Then I frosted the cupcakes and made the icing for them. I made chocolate and vanilla cupcakes and chocolate covered pretzel sticks with white chocolate candy melts and sprinkles. And I made a sign:

HELP KIDS LIKE ME FIGHT CANCER.
WATER AND BAKED GOODS FOR SALE.

I wanted to raise money for research for childhood cancer.

There's a gazebo in the middle of the town park, not far from our house. We set up a pop-up tent and a table and put all the treats on the table. My friends and I all made signs, and we stood out on the sidewalk holding them up:

HELP US HELP THEM — SADIE STRONG

In two and a half hours, we managed to raise $1,400 to donate to a cancer foundation called St. Baldrick's. People came from everywhere, some of them running to our booth. People out on walks or runs with their dogs would tear home and get their money and come back. People posted Facebook pictures with their cupcake and told followers to buy one. We didn't post prices; it was just by donation. Some people gave $100 and took a single cupcake, just one, even when I told them to take more.

We sold out of everything by 11:30 a.m. My friends and I managed to get one break to eat one cupcake apiece.

The next day I baked more, for clinic next week. I had never been busier in my life. But Mom and I were about to get busier—way, way busier. It began this way:

It was a regular day in early November and I was hanging out. I asked Mom, "Does Santa come to the hospital to give kids toys at Christmas?"

She said, "That's a great question. You should ask Dr. Engel."

I went to clinic a week later. Sitting on the examining table, I asked my doctor: "Do you know if Santa comes to the hospital on Christmas morning?"

"Yes, he does," Dr. Engel said. "Nurses tell me they see him walking around the halls in the middle of the night, bringing presents."

So I knew. But I thought, *That would be terrible to be in the hospital on Christmas.* It made me so sad. I love to spend Christmas with my family singing holiday songs, and I hated being in the hospital. Those kids must be feeling that, too. So I talked to Mom about it that night. "That's awful being in the hospital at Christmas. And Santa has the whole world to see, and so many kids on the floor. What if he can't get to them all? What if kids don't get all the toys they want? "So," I said. "What if we collect toys?"

Mom looked at me. "You mean a toy drive?"

"Yes. A toy drive."

"What would you want your goal to be? I mean, how many toys?"

I said, "I want to donate them to the hospital oncology floor at Children's. Let's just start off with 300 toys." Why 300? It's just a number that was speaking to me.

"Okay," she said. "Let's aim at that." But when she was alone with Dad, Mom said to him, "How on earth are we going to do that?"

We all sat around for a couple hours thinking about what to call the drive. We thought of catchy Christmas names: Sadie the Elf. Santa's Helper. Sadie's Toys. Then I said, "Sadie's Sleigh." You know, Santa's Sleigh. *Sadie's Sleigh.* It had a ring to it.

"That's perfect!" everybody said. And all the other ideas got thrown out.

All this time, we had been making videos about cancer and my chemo, and Mom was sharing my story on Facebook. We had a thousand followers. So, to promote Sadie's Sleigh, I made another video. "We're going to collect a bunch of toys," I said. "And we need your help."

Then right away, the day after the video, toys started pouring in. We put a shipping box on our porch, two feet high and four feet long, for people to drop toys into. We looked out the window and saw people running up, dropping off toys, and running off. It was like a reverse porch pirate. Instead of stealing packages, this time people were just appearing out of nowhere with toys and then disappearing.

Within a couple days, the shipping box was too small for all the toys that came in, so people started leaving toys on the side of the box. Three hundred toys landed on our porch in the first week. We kept the toys in Mom's office, now my art room. In our videos we updated people on the number of toys. After we hit our goal, we kept telling people we needed more.

I upped the goal to 500. And 200 more toys showed up.

"Okay. New number: 800." And we got 800.

"A thousand?"

It was December already, so that seemed pretty unlikely. And yet, we ended up with a total of 1,300 toys. A thousand more than what Mom thought might be an impossible goal.

I updated Dr. Engel and the nurses. Child Life helps deliver toys on Christmas, so we asked Caitlin and Dr. Engel if we were getting in the way. Caitlin said, "Some years we don't get enough toys, and we have to go shopping." So that made me feel better.

Katy Blakey, a Dallas TV reporter, had done a story after I made the video in the closet. And now she came again with a cameraman to report on Sadie's Sleigh. Then a moving company, Around the Clock Movers, reached out to the news station, who emailed us. The company offered to help in delivering the toys.

"That's perfect!" We didn't know how many cars we'd need. "We'd love the help." They still help, along with another company, Black Tie Moving. Now there are multiple delivery days.

We took a picture of all the toys in our office, but it didn't do the pile justice. We had to get a picture of all the toys laid out. Mom got Miss Cassie, the woman who dyed my hair, to help us set out all the toys in our driveway. We laid out a bunch of old sheets that morning to keep the toys clean. We had all the toys in trash bags, so the three of us hauled each bag, laying out one toy at a time like dominoes: each toy leaning on the next toy so you could see each one. It took us about three hours, not counting the time hauling everything out of the house.

Once all the toys were laid out, I stood in front of them with my arms out. I was still bald then. Mom got up on a small ladder and took a picture of me and all the toys. Then we loaded the toys back into the trash bags and hauled them back in.

The moving company came a couple days later, in mid-December. The toys filled up half of a giant moving truck. We followed it to the hospital, where all these people were waiting for us. They loaded the toys in big square laundry bins and put them in a storage unit.

Katy Blakey, the TV reporter, met us and did another story: "Now she's dropping them off!" That was December 17. The same day I gave the nurses and doctors candy canes filled with chocolate.

That Christmas, parents tagged us in the pictures of their kids with the presents. Dr. Engel had worked that day, so she got to see the kids get them. "You made them so happy," she said. "What you're doing has made such a difference for this Christmas."

But on Christmas Eve, I got the biggest present of all.

I was on treatment, which meant I wasn't allowed to hand out Sadie's Sleigh toys to the kids myself. I couldn't catch something or give them germs. Grant and I were upstairs watching YouTube.

"Hey, kids, come down here!"

We sat on the couch. Dad came through the back door with his arm behind his back.

Dad said, "I'm going to try not to cry. Grant, you've been the best brother, protecting your sister." Then he turned to me. "Sadie, you've been so strong through all this. Are you ready for your first Christmas present?"

In the middle of the speech, Grant started crying. He had seen the puppy.

Dad pulled a puppy dog from behind his back. He had a red ribbon around his neck. I ran over and picked him up, and Dad hugged Grant. I held the little furball. "I can't believe it!" I was so happy I couldn't cry. I'd been asking for a puppy forever. Mom came up with the name: Louie, after the designer Louis Vuitton.

Mom always gives Grant and me pajamas and a book to read on Christmas Eve. Louie was resting on my chest on the couch. I started reading to Louie. He was tired too, and he slept in his crate all night.

I always wake up early on Christmas. I woke up Mom and Dad. "It's Christmas! It's Christmas!" I went and got Louie.

I was on steroids, which makes you feel so terrible it's hard to sleep at night. So that morning after presents I lay down on a puffy chair in our living room. Louie curled up with me on my side, and we slept there for most of the morning.

The next year around September, we wondered whether to do Sadie's Sleigh again. We decided we had to. We didn't want any kids to go without presents. I increased the goal to 2,600, doubling what we got the previous year.

"Well, okay," Mom and Dad said.

I made lots of videos, and the toys starting coming in again. I also made an Amazon Wish List, and Grant and I picked a bunch of toys to add to the list. People from all over the country could order what they wanted, and the toys would be delivered to us. They could add a note to their gift. Every day after school, Amazon delivered boxes that were stacked to the top of our front door. One day I couldn't even get out the door! That year, 2016, we received 5,000 toys. We donated them to Cook Children's Medical Center in Fort Worth as well as my hospital, Children's Medical Center in Dallas.

That year, it took 20 volunteers, including Mom and me, to lay out the toys for a picture. The year after that, we had 40 or 50 volunteers. Last year, about a hundred. Sadie's Sleigh now gets tens of thousands of toys, and we box them all by category and stack them in our garage. Our driveway is too small for the picture, so everybody carries the boxes out to our cul-de-sac. We lay down a huge plastic tarp and announce it to people on Facebook. We have food for everybody and play Christmas music over big speakers loaned by a family friend. Little kids come to see the toys, which we take out of the boxes. The unpacking and laying out takes a hundred people about four hours. And then, just before Christmas, the moving companies show up. It takes them two trips, filling giant trucks.

But now some local businesses were asking whether we had a foundation. They wanted to donate money instead of toys, and have us do the shopping.

Mom said, "Yeah. Why aren't we a foundation?"

I said, "Yeah. Why not?" A foundation sounded like a really good idea. "We definitely should have a foundation!" Then I thought about it. "What's a foundation?"

Mom explained that a foundation—the official name is "charitable foundation"—is an organization that does good things with money. Mom and Dad had a friend help them with the paperwork, and the Sadie Keller Foundation got approved right before the 2016 Sadie's Sleigh.

The foundation gave us another idea. We thought: Why don't we do something all through the year, not just on Christmas? So right after we delivered the toys, we got together for another meeting and came up with the idea of Milestone Gifts. Childhood cancer fighters reach many milestones, like when they finish treatment. Or get out of the hospital after a long stay. Or finish radiation. Or go into remission, when the doctors can't find any more cancer. Or go back to school. They deserve a present. Still, we decided that a kid doesn't have to achieve a milestone to get a gift. Cancer kids sometimes just need something to cheer them up.

We made it so that parents can apply to our website. They ask for all kinds of stuff. They'll say, "Our kid loves dinosaurs and cars." So we might get both for that kid.

We give out a lot of Xboxes and Beats headphones, some little toys, some big things worth $300 or $400. We try to spend the same amount on each child. We get them sandboxes, bicycles, giant bounce houses, once a canoe, once a kayak, American Girl dolls, motorized vehicles they can ride—the little kids love that especially. Some kids want their bedroom to be redone. "I love unicorns." So a unicorn bedspread, unicorn lamps, unicorn pillows, and unicorn toys. We get them exactly what they've been wanting for so long and couldn't get on their own.

The great thing is, unlike Sadie's Sleigh, I get to give a lot of the gifts personally. The first Milestone Gift I delivered was a big dollhouse. It went to a little girl, three or four years old, named Avery. Her parents had said that Avery really wanted a dollhouse. When she finished her last chemo, we brought this ginormous dollhouse, super fancy, like a real house, to the hospital. We wheeled it on a wagon to her room. First, I went in without the wagon. Her parents knew I was coming, but Avery didn't. She was in bed, falling asleep when I came in. Chemo does that to you—it makes you super tired. Besides, it was pretty late in the day. I bent down and said, "Hey, Avery, how are you doing?"

She was sucking her thumb. Taking it out of her mouth, she said, "Fine."

"I think you're so strong and amazing for getting through this," I said. "So I have a surprise for you. Are you ready?"

Avery was sucking her thumb again. She nodded her head.

I went back out to the hall and rolled the wagon into her room. Her eyes went wide, and her thumb fell out of her mouth. She got right out of bed and went to the dollhouse. It was taller than she was. Now wide awake, Avery took the little people out of the dollhouse and started playing with them. Her parents stood in the room with big smiles.

I felt like my heart was ready to burst. This was better than Christmas, better than getting a big gift myself, almost as good as getting a puppy (though I wouldn't give up Louie for anything).

Since then, we've given more than 600 Milestone Gifts. I don't get to take them all to the kids myself. But I try to do it often, and the kids become my friends. Plus, I get to give gifts to kids who are already my best friends. One of them, Vara James, came to stay with us. She's my age, and she had just finished treatment when we gave her Beats headphones. She wears them all the time, even when she sleeps.

Another friend, Sadie Murata, got an iPhone case, a Nordstrom gift card for a shopping spree, and a little purse for her colostomy bag. A lot of things about cancer aren't painful, but they're still hard to go through or even talk about. It's one of the things you fight, and you have to keep a positive attitude. Sadie had a great attitude, and her purse looked amazing. Her parents called her Sadiebug, because she was little and cute and bright.

For those who don't live near me, the parents send videos of their kids getting the Milestone Gifts. Some of the kids are really little, and I can see them playing with their toys. They look right into the camera and smile and say, "Thank you, Sadie!" A lot of families share the videos and pictures on social media, and this made word spread fast all across the country.

At first, we did the shopping ourselves, going to Target or Best Buy to get exactly what the kids wanted. We would box the presents up, and I would write a note for every kid, on cards printed with my picture:

Hi, Liam, I think you're so strong. I hope you like your Milestone Gift from the Sadie Keller Foundation. Keep fighting! Love, Sadie

I wrote that kind of note to every fighter who got a gift. Some days we mailed out 20 gifts. My hand hurt from writing so much. But I thought it was important to give a personal touch. I wanted them to feel like I was there giving the gift myself. So I wrote what I would say to kids in person.

After a while, though, the number of gifts got out of control, and I just couldn't write personally to every kid. We now ship out a packet that tells kids their Milestone Gift is on the way. The packet includes a Sadie on a Stick, with a picture of my head on a stick like a lollipop. Kids always want to take a picture with me, so this lets them.

Other people help. Two women besides Mom are now on the board of directors of the Sadie Keller Foundation. Every few months, they come to our house and we have dinner and a meeting with Mom and Dad and my grandma. And we're about to add more people to the board. They all ask me for opinions on what we should do. And then we all make decisions together. I love how, although I'm only 12 years old, they treat me as if I was their age. They're one of the reasons I have gotten less shy around adults.

And the foundation also helped me make friends with tons of cancer kids. Which I loved. But some, including Sadie Murata and Vara, ended up making me sadder than I've ever been. And angrier, though it wasn't their fault. It wasn't at all their fault.

This is why I needed to fight for them, and for all the kids with cancer. The toys were making kids happy, but they weren't curing anybody. Mom kept looking up things about cancer, and she learned that only four percent of cancer research money was being spent on treating childhood cancer. Just four percent! We needed to do something. But I was just a kid. How was I going to do something about it?

Then along came more angels.

CHAPTER SEVEN

To Join the Battle, It Helps to Wear Pink

B efore I started fourth grade, Mr. Mike Gillette, a filmmaker with a cancer-fighting organization called The Truth 365, invited us to come to Washington, D.C., for CureFest. It's a two-day event that includes a march called Rally to the U. S. Capitol. I would have to skip school, but it seemed worth it. I hadn't been to D.C. since I was four, when we visited my grandma in Virginia. I didn't really remember that trip.

But just as we were making plans, Miss Annette Leslie texted Mom and asked if I could come to D.C. a week later. She wanted me to speak at the Golden Toast, which kicks off the Childhood Cancer Summit, a big Washington meeting of people who can make a difference. Miss Annette, who runs the cancer-fighting Carson Leslie Foundation, organizes the Golden Toast. It honors the four co-chairs of the Childhood Cancer Caucus in Congress. Congressman McCaul founded it. They're the people who fight for laws that fund our cause. "I don't just ask anybody," Miss Annette said. "It's really selective. The highlight of the night is the kid speaking."

"This sounds so great," Mom said. "But I don't know if we can stay the whole week. Sadie will have to skip the beginning of school." We were still new to the cancer community. I had only been diagnosed a year before. Besides, we weren't familiar with the Washington scene.

"It's a really big deal," Miss Annette said. "You should take this opportunity."

I decided I wanted to do it. This would be my first time speaking in front of people. But my first instinct is: *OK.*

Always before I speak, my heart starts racing. It's better than it was that first time, because I've spoken in public more than 50 times since then. But I'm still nervous, even when I tell myself I'll do fine. There's always the possibility you can mess up. Still, in the end, I figure I'm a kid. People will cut me slack. They'll let me get away with mistakes. So my nerves don't really matter.

I mean, think about it. You can say to yourself, "I'm just a kid. I'm not very good at speaking." And people will say, "She's just a kid. That's really brave." Even if you look shy and the words won't come quickly, people will root for you. At least, that's been my experience.

The four of us flew to Washington and stayed in a hotel a few blocks from the White House. Next morning, we showed up at the nearby Freedom Plaza for a meet and greet. The organizers had set up tables with poster board and markers. Everybody was making signs for the rally. I made one with a gold ribbon for childhood cancer and the words:

I'M WORTH MORE THAN 4%

I wanted people to know about that four percent—the portion out of billions of dollars of cancer research that goes to childhood cancers. There are 12 types of cancer that kids can get, along with a hundred or so sub-types. Some of them have a survival rate of zero. That's a death sentence. There isn't enough money for scientists to make the best chemotherapy for all of them, drugs that would save kids' lives.

When I finished my sign, people started coming up to me. They had seen my closet videos. I started feeling like I was a part of things.

We lined up, led by a man with a shaved head and earrings and lots of tattoos. Everyone calls him Tattoo Tom. He was a single dad when his daughter, Shayla, died of cancer, and he started a foundation called StillBrave. Tattoo Tom has a really loud voice, which is why he walks in front of the rally. He has a bullhorn, but sometimes it seems like he doesn't need it. He's that loud.

We marched from Freedom Plaza to the Capitol while Tattoo Tom had us all chanting:

> Kids with cancer got it rough!
> *Kids with cancer got it rough!*
> Don't you look the other way!
> *Don't you look the other way!*
> You might be marching with us some day!
> *You might be marching with us some day!*

Mom, Dad, Grant and I all looked at each other while we yelled and carried our signs. Never in a million years did we think we would be doing anything like this. We're just not the protesting type of people. We never thought we'd be rallying for childhood cancer in Washington, D.C. Then again, we never thought we'd be a family with childhood cancer. Besides, the First Amendment to the Constitution is not just about freedom of speech. It also protects freedom of assembly: the right to march behind a tattooed guy with a bullhorn.

As we marched, we looked behind us. I saw hundreds of people walking and in wheelchairs: parents who had lost their child, advocates for childhood cancer, all kinds of organizations, siblings of kids with cancer. And kids like me with cancer. A lot of kids had no hair. Like me. It felt so good to see them. I felt like all of us belonged together.

We went on to the National Mall and made a huge circle. Mr. Mike came up to me. "Sadie, would you like to say a few things?"

"Sure." I thought, *Here I go again, always saying yes.* I had no idea what I would say.

Five minutes later, I found myself standing in the middle of the huge circle of people, all staring at me. Mr. Mike handed me a mike.

I had no words. And then I did.

"I'm Sadie Keller. I have leukemia. We're here to be loud. To fight for childhood cancer and all the kids. I'm so happy to be here this year."

Everyone screamed *WOO HOO!!!*

I smiled and gave the mike back to Mr. Mike.

I walked back to my family like I was floating. "Good job," Mom said.

I still don't know how I did that. It may not rank up there with the greatest speeches ever made in Washington, but I was eight years old and had never spoken to so many people. Now I knew I could. And ever since then, every time I speak, I sort of leave myself. I just start talking. The words just come.

After the rally, everyone walked back to Freedom Plaza. There were tents set up, each with a table offering temporary tattoos. There was a photo booth, and there was an area with tiny stuffed animals the size of your palm—elephants, pigs, that sort of thing. You adopt them and get a birth certificate.

It seemed like Mr. Mike was everywhere that weekend. He already felt like a friend. We first met him when he heard about my closet video and visited us in Dallas. He filmed an interview with me about my thoughts on cancer. "Why do you think people don't like to talk about childhood cancer?"

I said, "Because they're scared, and they don't want to see anybody with it. They don't want to talk about it, and they don't want to deal with it. I feel like they should start talking about it so we can raise awareness. Awareness leads to money for research so we can find better cures for childhood cancer. I want to start talking about it to spread awareness."

Then I'm guessing he wanted me to feel more comfortable, so he mixed in some funny comments and questions to lighten things up. "We work with two other Sadies," he said. "Don't you think that three would be too many? From now on, I would like for you to introduce yourself as Katie Seller."

I laughed. "Sure!" but after a while I asked him if I could be Katie Seller for only a little while and then go back to Sadie. I like my name. It's who I am. Still, I liked Mr. Mike right away. He likes to joke, and I'm on to his pranks.

At CureFest, Mr. Mike kept bringing people over. I kept thinking he would introduce me as Katie Seller, but he used my real name, even when he had me meet another Sadie: Sadie Murata. A couple years older though we were the same size, she was in a wheelchair and looked pale and thin, and she was bald like me. She had her arms around a heated, weighted bear she called Sickie Bear. It made her feel better when she held it against her tumor.

Later on, as I got to know her, I found Sadie to be really funny and super nice. But here in the tent at the rally, we were both shy.

The next day we did a Three Sadies photo shoot. Mr. Mike would say, "Sadie, your arm is a little awkward. Move it a little," and all three of us would move our arms. Our moms were laughing all through it.

Sadie turned out to be a lot like me. She never complained and always looked happy, even though she kept relapsing again and again. It seemed like she never got to finish chemo.

The evening that Sadie Murata and I met, I got to meet another girl who became one of my best friends: Vara James. She was my age and was bald like me, still in treatment. She had Wilms tumor—kidney cancer. All the moms bonded, and all the kids bonded. That's one thing about having cancer as a child. You make the most amazing friends ever because you've been through the same things and can relate. There's an understanding. We share funny stories.

With my friend Vara, we share things like: "One time my nurse did this weird thing...." We talk about the feeling of different chemos, or how terrible some of them taste. "Oh my gosh, they do!" Or: "Whenever people say 'What happened to your hair?' it makes me so annoyed."

Vara lives in Michigan. She visited our house much later. We made a video about certain super annoying things that people ask about cancer. We made each other laugh. My favorite song at the time was "Bohemian Rhapsody." I've been a Queen fan forever. The song came on the radio in the car and we started singing it. Miss Emily, Vara's Mom, said, "You should rewrite the words."

"Yeah!" Vara and I both said.

So we did a video for our rewritten song:

> *Is this my real life? Is this a bad dream?*
> *I caught a disease and had no idea what*
>   *was happening....*
> *Mama, I know you want to cry.*
> *If I'm not gonna be here tomorrow,*
> *Please carry on, carry on.*
> *Because cancer doesn't matter.*

In the video we're smiling and having a great time, and we end the song playing air guitar on the floor. This may seem weird to you, but the horribleness of cancer becomes...not normal exactly, but something every cancer fighter *faces*. Something she can even joke about, and which other cancer fighters can find funny, even if people who don't have to deal with cancer can't find anything

90

funny about it. This is one big reason why kids with cancer become best friends with each other.

But that video came later, after Vara and I met in Washington.

Right after CureFest, I met another special friend, Lily Weaver. Mr. Mike introduced us. I was feeling especially shy, because Lily was 14, which seemed really old. Six years older than I was. But she took me off away from our parents, and we sat on a bench and talked, and then suddenly it was like we were the same age. She did most of the talking, to be honest, which was a good thing. She asked me about school and my treatments, and suddenly we were best friends. Here's the thing about Lily: She smiled all the time. She wouldn't stop smiling. And this was a girl with Ewing's sarcoma, an especially nasty and painful kind of cancer. Just 200 to 250 children and teenagers are diagnosed each year, and it's even rarer in females. You can get terrible pain in your bones, and the long-term survival rate is somewhere around 50 percent—though some scientists say it's closer to 20 or 30 percent. Nobody really knows about long-term survival in childhood cancer. Most doctors and scientists stop counting after five years. Some kids do okay for five years and then die of the side effects of treatment, or of weak immune systems, and their death gets blamed on non-cancer causes—even if they'd probably be alive today if it weren't for the cancer.

Anyway, think about being a girl who just wants to graduate from high school someday but has to go through all the pain and chemo and radiation. That was Lily, who was always smiling. People think of cancer kids as being victims. We talk about ourselves as fighters. One way to fight is to do the opposite of acting like victims, which is smiling. And when I met Lily, she had the biggest smile I had ever seen. Which made her the best fighter I had met.

I learned from Lily that happiness isn't just a mood that's given to you. It's a skill. And childhood cancer fighters have to be best of all at that skill. Meeting Lily was like meeting the best of the best. Her smile was making everybody around her happy, including me.

Lily cheered me up all through my treatment. Every time I went in to the clinic for chemo, she would text me, telling me how much she missed me and how she was there for me in spirit. That was Lily. She made everyone around her happy.

I met other amazing people that first week in Washington. Mr. Mike introduced me to Tatum Foster, a Ewing's sarcoma girl about my age. Unlike me, Tatum loved wearing wigs. Her favorite was bright pink. "My name means cheerful," she said.

The night of the Golden Toast, we met with Miss Annette. I had my speech ready on a notecard. This was my first scheduled speech on a stage, in the Library of Congress. Miss Annette introduced me to Congressman Michael McCaul, a tall man with gray hair, wearing a suit and tie. He looked like a congressman from the movies. I was wearing a really colorful short dress, and he noticed it. "Your dress is so pretty!" he said. "And I love your headband." He had to bend down to talk to me. I was really short, and he's a big man.

I gave my speech, and then Congressman McCaul got up to speak. "I chair the Homeland Security Committee," he said. "And my job is to protect the American people from threats facing the nation. He pointed out that cancer is the number one killer of kids by disease. "I can't think of anything more important than saving a child's life."

Congresswoman Jackie Speier from California was there as well, and I got to meet her. I felt like a VIP.

Congressman McCaul came up to me after they spoke. I told him about the video I made, and he listened to me like I was the most important person in the room. Then Nancy Goodman of Kids v Cancer came up to me. "I know you're going to do something huge," she said. "You're going to do big things. I want to be the first person to get your autograph. Will you sign my business card?"

I had never given my autograph before.

Miss Nancy turned to Mom. "I would love to work with Sadie if you and she are interested."

We definitely were. And the following spring, Miss Nancy arranged for us to lobby on Capitol Hill. You think of lobbyists as people in expensive suits. But anyone can lobby. Still, it helps to have a lot of people supporting you—a cause with supporters who really care.

I wore a pink dress and a really nice headband. It would have been a hairband if I'd had any hair. One of the offices we visited was the one for Congressman McCaul. He was about to do an interview with Julie Fine of NBC's

Dallas station. Julie works with my friend Katy Blakey at the same station, so she knew who I was. She and the Congressman asked if I wanted to do the interview with him.

"Sure," I said. Only this time I meant it. I had done other interviews at that point, so I knew what to expect. I explained why I was lobbying, and the Congressman talked about the bills he was trying to get passed.

When the TV crew left, we spent half an hour with Congressman McCaul, which is a lot of time for someone that busy. Then he said, "What are you guys doing for the rest of the day?"

Mom said, "We have a few more appointments. But after that, nothing."

"Have you ever seen the floor of the House?"

"No, we haven't, but we'd love it!" Mom said.

What? A floor? Of a house? I had already seen plenty of floors in houses, so it seemed weird that Mom should get all excited about this. Couldn't the Congressman show me something cool?

"Can you come back after your meetings?" he said. "I would love to show Sadie around the Capitol."

Oh. He meant the floor of the House, capital H. As in, the House of Representatives. "Yes," I said. "That would be so cool!"

After our meetings, we came back and he took off the whole afternoon, cancelling all his other appointments. He took Mom and me on a tour of the whole Capitol, along with Jennifer Flynn (she works with Nancy Goodman at Kids v Cancer), and Mr. Mike Gillette from The Truth 365.

He pointed out some of the paintings that hang on the walls throughout the Capitol building. It wasn't like an art tour. It was more like a funny history lesson: "Look how he's stepping on the other guy's foot," he said about one painting. It showed Thomas Jefferson's foot on top of John Adams's foot, which made me laugh. Here was one of the most important people I had ever met, now ranking member of the Foreign Affairs Committee. He had been around the world on the nation's business. There are laws, big laws, passed because of him. And here he was acting just like a friend.

He took me out onto the Speaker's Balcony. That was part of the office of the Speaker of the House of Representatives, a very powerful person. We walked out onto it, and there was this amazing view of the Washington Monument and all the other buildings, all shining in the sun. This didn't seem real. It all looked like a painting.

The Congressman pointed out the different buildings. And then he said, "You know, Sadie, you can do anything."

But I wasn't thinking about how I could do anything someday. I was doing something now: I was lobbying. In the U.S. Capitol. With a congressman who was taking the afternoon off just for me. It was almost too much to be true.

"See this line in the middle of the balcony?"

I looked down, and there was a line right down the middle of the stone.

"If you stand on the line and look toward the Washington Monument, you'll be on both sides of the Capitol. On one side is the House, and on the other is the Senate."

I put my hands on the balcony rail and stood with my feet on either side of the line.

Then he took me back down to the middle of the Capitol, in the very center where the Rotunda is. It looks really fancy, with little statues showing American history. At the very top is a painting showing George Washington ascending to Heaven.

Congressman McCaul pointed to the middle of the Rotunda. "If you look up and you spin, you get really dizzy."

"What?"

"Come here. I'll show you." He held both my hands and we began to spin while looking up at George Washington ascending to Heaven. He was right. I did get really dizzy. But I didn't throw up, which would have been so embarrassing.

And that was the beginning of our friendship. When he was in Dallas with his daughter, visiting her at Southern Methodist University, I gave Congressman McCaul a painting I made of me curled up in the hospital. "The colors show how I turned a bad experience into a positive one," I told him. I also gave him a copy of my painting of a friend who passed away. I had painted angel wings on her to show she was in Heaven. He got choked up looking it. Then he asked if we wanted a tour of the campus. His wife's foundation, the Mays Family Foundation, had made a donation to the Sadie Keller Foundation. "Come meet with me, and I'll present this check," he said. We met him at the SMU campus. A reporter was there, and they did an interview. Afterward, the Congressman gave me and my family a full-on tour of SMU. After seeing everything there, I want to go to SMU for my college. Besides, it's close to my family. Maybe the college will let me stay at home.

Congressman McCaul and I text and call each other a lot. When we go to D.C., he invites us to his house for pizza and to talk. His house is on Capitol Hill and his balcony has a view of the Capitol Building. We've gone to dinner with him in New York when we did national television one year. We hung out and it was super fun. Last year at CureFest, we visited his house three nights in a row.

He's always excited to see me. We laugh a lot and talk about what I've been doing for the summer or what's my next big idea for childhood cancer. I showed him pictures of a trip to Australia—thanks to the Make-A-Wish Foundation, which gives sick kids their biggest dreams. The Congressman showed us a video of him and his family in Africa. He likes to tell us stories about his dad, who was a bomber in World War II.

His office is like a museum, with lots of historical objects. I asked what was his very favorite thing. He had to think about it for a while. Then he said, "Well, my daughter made me this picture frame that opens into another picture." It's a picture of his daughter Jewel and him.

Congressman McCaul is my teammate. We do a lot of stuff together to help pass laws. He's the one who has helped get important bills passed. He inspires me to do more. I love to do interviews with him. And he's always around when we come to Washington to lobby.

What's the deal about lobbying? It's how you get Congress to pass those bills. Someone has an idea. Then someone writes it up into a bill—often lobbyists themselves do. The bills I've lobbied for were written by childhood cancer advocates. Then we get together to promote the bill and spread the ideas to members of Congress.

Usually I lobby with just my mom. I prefer that because, while I love doing it with groups, I can speak freely when it's just us. Usually I see five or six members of Congress, with the appointments made by Kids v Cancer. Mom and I stay in a hotel on Capitol Hill and take a taxi to the Rayburn Building, the office building for the U.S. House of Representatives. You have to go through security. It's kind of like airport security, but sometimes the line goes out to the sidewalk with people waiting on the stairs. Sometimes there's no line at all.

After going through security, we go up three stairs and hang a right. That's where Congressman McCaul's office is—2001 Rayburn. We always stop and take a picture in front of his sign. Then we head to the cafeteria to get settled. We decide what I'm going to say about my story, then get to the bill. Mom and I usually don't eat anything; we get a seat and just talk. Do I want to talk about the hard times I've been through, or just discuss the bill? That way I know what to say, and in which order.

The amount of time you get with a member of Congress really depends. It might be as short as ten minutes, or as long as 45. We go to both the Senate and the House. Some of the people we have seen the most include the staff for Congressman Michael Burgess from Texas, Congressman Mike Kelly from Pennsylvania, Senator Bob Casey from Pennsylvania, and Senator Johnny Isakson from Georgia, whose son is involved with a childhood cancer foundation. Also Congresswoman Rosa DeLauro from Connecticut, who has amazing purple hair.

I sometimes lobby with other kids. One of the special times, I did it with Lily Weaver. I wanted to introduce her to all the members of Congress and the staffers I had met in earlier years. Things just seemed to go better with her along. We shared the scary stuff that happens with cancer and told the staffers why we need more funding. But in between our meetings, we had fun being together.

When I lobby with my mom, we often meet with a staffer who will then go to the congressman and say, "You have to meet this girl."

Here's what I told them when I was lobbying for the STAR Act:

"I'm Sadie Keller. I'm 12 years old. When I was seven, I was diagnosed with cancer. I had to go through two and a half years of hard chemotherapy treatment. Throughout those years, I went through terrifying procedures and side effects. The first month I was diagnosed, my port got infected, and it had to be taken out, and it looks like I've been shot. One of the most terrifying experiences was a rare side effect from the methotrexate in my spine. I had stroke-like symptoms. My arm felt like it was floating, and I couldn't speak. My mom had to rush me to the hospital not knowing what was going on. I had a CAT scan and an MRI, and it was really scary. I'm here because I know what kids are going through."

Then I went: "Did you know that only four percent of funding of cancer research goes to childhood cancer? Kids are the future, and there are many types of cancers, some with no survival rate at all. Without these kids, there isn't a future.

"There's a bill called the STAR act, which stands for Survivorship, Treatment, Access, and Research. Survivorship is a really big part of this bill, because there aren't a lot of treatments that have enough of a survivor rate. If this bill gets passed, we can get treatments for these kids. It gives the scientists more money to find cures with chemo that doesn't have long-term side effects."

Some of the staffers didn't know what to do. They were kind of awkward with kids and said things like, "Okay, wow! You're very brave. That's a very amazing story you have." Staffers tend to be really young; some look like they're still in college. Some didn't know what to say at all, just "Thank you."

Other staffers said, "I didn't know about that. Tell me more about the four percent." Or, "Tell me more about what you went through."

Lobbying is really important. It's something I love to do, because these children need someone's help. I want to be a voice for kids who don't have a voice. That's what lobbying is: It gives a voice for others. I do it because I can offer something different from many lobbyists. Congress members and their staffers see many, many adults every single day. But when a kid comes in to explain something so hard to talk about, that's really special. It makes these people think, *These kids are real.*

I'm not just some random kid. I'm a kid who actually went through cancer. They hear that children really need help, and they hear it from the child. Another great thing about being a child lobbyist: You meet other kids like you, who have been through a Hard Time and want to help others. I've met the most amazing kids. Including Lily.

In the spring of 2017, Lily and I did a video for The Truth 365 in which we took the Bean Boozled Jelly Bean Challenge, eating jelly beans where you didn't know the flavors. It's worth watching on YouTube if you ever get a chance. Just search for The Truth 365 and Bean Boozled. You'll see how puffy my face was from the steroids, and how bald I was. Lily looked beautiful with short hair that was growing back, and she had her always-there smile on her face. Lily was already a star among cancer fighters. A couple years after I met her, she did an HBO documentary with the famous boxer Jarrell Miller.

Our Bean Boozled Challenge was really different. It showed how normal cancer kids can be. We spun a wheel that chose which jelly bean each of us had to eat. Each bean may have one of two flavors. A yellowish bean could be either buttered popcorn or rotten egg. A pink one was dead fish or strawberry-banana smoothie. A white one was spoiled milk or coconut. And there were a bunch more. We spun the dial and got "caramel corn or moldy cheese." Lily got moldy cheese. I spat mine out so fast I didn't know what I got. We spat into cups that said "More than 4%" on them, reminding viewers of the need to spend more than four percent of cancer research on childhood cancer. (Though I also spat all over my hand.) In another spin, Lily got lime and I got lawn clippings. It tasted like water from a public pool. "You know like when you go near the little kids?" I said. Lily tilted her head back and laughed really hard with her eyes closed, and I laughed harder than I've laughed in my entire life.

In the beginning of the jelly bean video, Lily introduced herself as "cancer survivor Lily." But just a few months later, we learned that Lily had relapsed. We visited her and gave her Milestone Gifts: Beats headphones and a Sephora makeup kit. Lily was amazing at doing makeup.

Lily and I did another Truth 365 shoot, showing the two of us arm wrestling. She won, but it took a while! We both look skinny and weak in that video, but when you saw us wrestle you would think we were really strong.

Then Mr. Mike took what may be the most famous picture of Lily and me. It's called Trading Places. Our moms had found a beautiful photo of two sisters. One had her head down, looking sad. The other stood behind her, comforting her. We were going to pose Lily comforting me, since she was older and had done that all through my treatment. "I want to be the girl with her head down," I told Mr. Mike.

He said, "How about Lily instead?" After all, she was the one who had relapsed.

"Oh, yeah." Now I was the one comforting Lily. I was texting her before her scans, telling her I was praying for her. We had been trading roles over the year.

The problem was, I was much shorter than Lily. So Mr. Mike got a pile of shirts and a roll of tape and I stood on tippy toes on the pile. The photo is beautiful and sad. It shows me standing behind Lily, with my hand on her elbow. Lily is bald, and she covers her face. I look very serious. But if you were there for the shoot, you would have seen me fall off the pile again and again. It was really awkward to balance on the pile and keep my hands over Lily's elbows. Our moms kept cracking up, and so did we. Mr. Mike had to keep doing retake after retake. "Okay," he kept saying. "Childhood cancer serious!" Which just made us laugh more.

I wish the two of us could laugh forever. But things turned out to be very different.

CHAPTER EIGHT

The Summer of Love and Anger

Two and a half years after my diagnosis, when I was ten years old, I got my last spinal tap and the last medicine through my port. A few of my favorite nurses came to see me reach this huge milestone, even though they weren't working that day. A big tradition at many hospitals is to ring a bell when you finish chemo. My hospital didn't have one, so we brought our own. Mom had it made specially for me, with a cool plaque. We went to an area of the hospital that wasn't being used that day, and I got to ring it where it wouldn't bother any of the other patients. I felt like...like I had run a hundred thousand marathons. Like I had swum across the ocean. We had spent so many holidays on chemo. I had missed so much school. I had been poked hundreds of times, had 19 procedures, had taken thousands of pills. (As for the pills: I still needed to take a jillion more over the next couple of weeks. But even that finally ended.)

While we waited for that last spinal, I went to a room where Hunter, a high school senior with lymphoma, was getting *his* last spinal. I brought him a Milestone Gift: wireless Beats headphones. It made the day seem even more like a celebration.

The fun kept going. The following week, everyone at my elementary school wore Sadie shirts or the color green, my favorite color then. They put up a giant banner that everyone signed. And I told my story to the whole fourth grade. This made me feel a part of things again. It had been a long time since I felt like a normal kid, with hair and everything.

Meanwhile, we were planning a huge No More Chemo party where I could thank all the people who had helped me over those years. But just when it seemed like life just couldn't get better, we found out that Hunter, the boy I had given the headphones to, was back in the hospital. Doctors were trying to find out why he was in terrible pain. (He's in remission and in college today.) Then even more horrible news came: My friend Tatum was diagnosed with a secondary cancer. It was caused by all the treatments for her first cancer. Tatum had to get a bone marrow transplant and lots more chemo, just when we thought she was done with all that. We'd had so much fun together filming with Mr. Mike, just being goofy together with wigs to cover our bald heads.

At my No More Chemo party, all kinds of childhood cancer fighters and survivors came. I spoke and then asked them all to come up. When I asked for a round of applause, the crowd went wild. They knew what we had learned: Even survivors still have to fight. They still have long-term effects from the chemo. They still wonder if the cancer will come back. It never ends.

Two days later, I was washing my hair when I looked at my hands. They were full of hair. I was done with chemo! This wasn't supposed to happen! So I asked Dad to shave my head for the eighth time. Soon after that, I got a nasty rash on my head, neck and chest. It hurt really bad, especially on my head where the follicles got infected. And it itched like crazy. Plus, I got weird bumps under the skin of my left hand. They hurt when I touched them. It still was happening, this whole cancer extravaganza. It didn't feel like I had stopped treatment. I didn't feel different. But even then, at least for the moment, I knew I was one of the lucky ones. I was in remission. For now. My hair would grow back. I would get healthier. There was a good chance that the cancer would never ever ever come back.

And there was always the chance that it would.

Just a few days after losing my hair again, we went back to the clinic for my first big checkup since I finished chemo. Parents of a lot of childhood cancer fighters talk about *scanxiety*—wondering if the next scan from a CT or MRI machine will show cancer. With leukemia kids like me, though, it's all about the blood, not scans. I have to get my blood drawn and checked for cancer cells. And then we pray until we get the results.

When the results came, we all breathed out. No cancer. Still in remission.

But as if cancer had to remind me that it was always lurking like some horrible beast just around the corner, my dear friend Vara had a relapse. She was the girl with Wilms tumor, the one I sang with for our cancer version of "Bohemian Rhapsody." The one with headphones around her neck all the time. The funny, happy, always singing girl. Her tumor was growing, and the doctors were running out of options.

That was also when Lily Weaver had relapsed. And about the same time, we learned that our friend Sadie Murata, Sadiebug, the Other Sadie, had taken a turn for the worse. She had had one relapse after another, and things looked bad. We had worked together on many projects for Mr. Mike and The Truth 365.

When Mom told me the news of Vara and Lily and Sadie, I didn't cry. I just got mad. I clenched my fists and breathed deeply. *This can't happen. This just has to stop.* I felt like screaming.

It wasn't over. It would never be over for some of us. But it can end for future kids. It has to end.

That same week, we had a happier day. Mom and I delivered a Milestone Gift to Benjamin, a 13-year-old boy who's now ten years cancer-free from medulloblastoma. That's a horrible kind of brain cancer. He had to get brain surgery, lots and lots of radiation, and high-dose chemo. That all cured his cancer, but the treatments left him blind and partially deaf. And he had to have major back and neck surgery, years after his treatments ended. When we visited him, he was rubbing his eyes. "I'm wiping the blind out of my eyes," he said. But when I gave him an iPad that has voice command, he gave me a hug, and then he held my hands. Benjamin's mom told me about when he found out he had cancer. He was just five years old, and he was playing baseball. He got a great hit and was running fast when he suddenly fell at second base. He got carried back to the dugout and taken to the hospital. Cancer.

That whole summer, the summer when I was ten, was filled with the highest highs and the lowest lows. It's as though a whole life got squooshed into a couple months, with big wins and terrible losses and good news and the worst news, when I was feeling such love and then so much terror. I was still on that roller coaster that refuses to go in a circle, that just goes on promising a destination that gets farther and farther away.

June 30 was one of the good days. We visited the cutest three-year-old, little Sierra. She had just finished her treatment for Ewing's sarcoma, a bone cancer at the base of her skull. The tumor had wrapped around the blood vessels behind her eyes and nose, which meant that surgeons couldn't operate on it without killing her. It grew down into her sinuses, putting pressure on the nerves to the eyes. This made her blind just when she had started chemo. She woke and screamed for her daddy to fix her eyes. But when she finished radiation, she found that she could see a little—shapes and light. The doctors were amazed. We gave Sierra the toy she wanted most: a giant Enchancian Castle, with some Sofia the First dolls. She sat in my lap and kept showing her family all of her new toys. My heart felt fit to burst.

And then back to getting my blood drawn. With three of my friends relapsing, Mom started freaking out a little. She had kept it together for years. But now she was wondering: Would I make it to the official leukemia goal of staying cancer-free ten years after treatment? She kept wondering to herself: *Why is she sleeping so much? Why is she so tired? Why is she getting so thin? What about those nasty rashes? Her eyes look different; are those black circles?*

After that, an up day. My family and I got invited to Las Vegas! The Truth 365 and Dance Hope Cure asked me to speak at the Velocity Dance convention and competition. It lasts ten days with the most amazing dancing. I got up to speak in front of more than 1,500 people. I had written down what I wanted to say, and then I rewrote it a lot and practiced it over and over and over. I was feeling nervous backstage. Grant was beside my mom, and as I began to walk onto the stage, he whispered, "Come on, Sadie!"

Love makes you brave.

Plus, the crowd was so unbelievably supportive. When I said that I had finished chemo just six weeks before, the crowd just roared! And at the end, they gave a standing ovation. I don't think it was for me exactly. Well, it was, but also for what my voice stood for. They were clapping and yelling for all the kids who had been so brave, the ones who got through the cancer. And the ones who fought and still didn't make it. They were cheering for all the angels.

That same summer, I went back to physical therapy. I kept tripping whenever I tried to walk normally. The chemo had tightened up my Achilles tendon so much that it caused my feet to drop, and I lost my arches. My ankles turned in. But I was getting stronger, and now that I wasn't on steroids the swelling in my face and the rest of my body was going down. And my hair was growing back! Such a big up.

Followed by a down. My friend Tony Colton died that summer. We had spent time with him and his family at a gala held by the famous sportscaster Dick Vitale for the

V Foundation. Tony was one of the nicest people there, always smiling. He had a beautiful girlfriend, Vanessa. So unfair.

And another down. Ariella Stein, age 11, passed away from Ewing's sarcoma. Mr. Mike had introduced us at Curefest, and she and Lily were really close. Ariella had the same thought I had about sick kids needing happiness. She started a foundation, Ari's Bears, with her own money to deliver stuffed bears to kids in hospitals.

The same day that Ariella died, Lily relapsed for the second time. Lily! The girl who seemed my same age even though she was older—the girl I did the Jelly Bean Challenge with! She had been five years Off Treatment when she relapsed for the first time. Five years OT! And she was off chemo for only six months before she relapsed this second time. How was this possible? Lily was supposed to be going into her junior year of high school. She was supposed to be getting her driver's license and thinking about where she wanted to go to college. Instead, she was back in the hospital. She had told Mr. Mike after he took our Trading Places photo, "I don't understand why kids keep facing cancer. Isn't once enough?" Lily and Vara, two of my closest friends, relapsed just a week apart. We called ourselves the Three Little Pigs, the Three Amigos, the Three Musketeers. Now they had cancer again, and I didn't. For now.

It was the summer of love and anger.

And, for me, more tests. Some swelling that I was experiencing seemed to be some sort of allergic reaction. Not cancer. My blood sugar dropped, so I had to eat every few hours. I was dropping weight like crazy, a whole pound in a few days. All while eating like a pig.

So I didn't have cancer, but things were still wrong. We thought we were done with talking about the side effects of the drugs. I mean, I wasn't on chemo! But now we weren't talking cancer fighting. We were talking survivorship. The doctors and nurses kept handing Mom sheets of long-term effects from the drugs I wasn't taking anymore. Because of the steroid dexamethasone, they have to watch my bones because they may break more easily. The other drugs bring their own issues. Vincristine: hard on the heart. Methotrexate: brain problems maybe, and learning disabilities. (I'm not great at math, but that could just be me, not the chemo.) Cyclophosphamide: hard on the liver. The drugs and the cancer made me grow more slowly. My weight today lies at the twelfth percentile, meaning 88 percent of other girls my age weigh more than I do. Before cancer, I was right on the average. I'm at fifteenth percentile in height.

After four years of appointments and talking about the labs and my blood counts and watching for cancer, Mom had gotten used to looking at all the reports and steeling herself for each visit. We fought hard and got through it all. And now we were meeting with a nurse practitioner who was new to us, part of the survivorship program. She was going through all the long-term side effects and we were looking at each other like, *What???* They have to watch my heart now?

I call myself a survivor, but that doesn't mean I'm past cancer. I'm just in remission. Maybe you should call me a remissionary.

Some cancer kids don't like the word "survivor" at all. It gives the wrong impression. People think you don't ever have to get poked again. They think you don't have to keep going to the clinic every few months to see whether the cancer has come back. I'll have to get checkups every year for the rest of my life. And remember how Lily called herself a survivor in our Bean Boozled Challenge? She had been off treatment for five years, and the doctors had found no cancer. She had a big Five Years Cured party. Then a couple months later she started having pain in her bones that wouldn't go away. The cancer was back. That's how fast it can change.

In the clinic, I got more pokes, more blood tests for my thyroid, heart, liver, everything. My immune system had dropped, making any germs dangerous for me. And the next day I was supposed to start fifth grade. Mom kept hugging me like she needed hugs more than I did.

I did go back to school. I kept doing my art and baking and gearing up for Sadie's Sleigh. And the summer ended. But the roller coaster didn't.

In mid-September, we went to visit the Other Sadie, Sadie Murata, to say goodbye. She was getting hospice at home, her life drawing to an end. Mom had gotten really close to Sadie's mom. When we got to her house, Sadie was lying on the living room couch, in and out of sleep. Her older brother and sister and her parents were in the room with her. They weren't going to lose a moment of her life. The family had just gotten a dog, a cute fat chihuahua named Juan Solo. When Sadie woke up, we talked about Juan and the other things she loved. Then I hugged her. "I love you, Sadie," I said. "See you soon."

Two weeks later, Mom told me that Sadiebug had gone to Heaven. She had passed away in her father's arms. She was 12 years old. "I'm so mad!" I yelled. But I took a breath and said, "I'm glad she isn't in pain anymore." And I was glad she was in Heaven, all healed.

After a few days I started worrying about all the other fighters I knew. "If anything ever happens to Lily and Vara," I told Mom, "I don't know what I'm going to do."

But I focused on Sadie Murata with my art. I needed to paint her. Art is therapeutic for me; I find it calming to paint what's in my head. And I would rather celebrate a person's life than mourn her. So I took a canvas and drew a picture of the two of us together. I made her an angel, showing both of us from the back. We're holding hands, and Sadie has wings. On one of the wings I drew a ladybug. Then I sponged a bunch of colors, green and blue and red and yellow, all around to represent the world with childhood cancer. I took some white and gold and put it on the side of the canvas. That's Heaven. And I painted a gold ribbon on the left corner. We framed it and hung it up in my room. That picture means a lot to me. But first we made a photocopy and brought it to Sadie's family when we went back to Virginia for her celebration of life. A huge crowd was there. It was sad, but a beautiful reminder of who she was. We all released a bunch of ladybug balloons.

So much love. So much anger.

In late September, I finally got my port out. It had been my lifeline for chemo, blood and platelet transfusions, everything that killed the cancer and kept me alive. The night before the operation, Mom and Dad and Grant took turns rubbing my port for good luck. It was the only time I had let anybody but doctors and nurses touch it. And then...just a scar. One I'm very proud of.

The winter brought more sad news, with more friends relapsing. The mom of one of the kids, Lilly Armbruster, shared her pain on Facebook. "I have HOPE again tonight (like I did last night and the night before) that in the morning I will see her big brown eye looking at me and I get 1 more time to hear her say 'I love you too.'" Lilly had rhabdomyosarcoma, the same kind of cancer as Sadie Murata. She was little and cute, younger than me. She passed away the following spring just a few months after she attended my End of Chemo party. Her mother held her hand and watched her take her last three breaths. "She looked so beautiful," her mother wrote on Facebook.

It's hard to lose a friend when you're a kid. It's hard to lose a bunch of friends to cancer. But I can't begin to imagine how hard it is for the mother.

My own mother can imagine. She has imagined it ever since I got diagnosed. I guess she'll be imagining it forever. But we're the lucky ones.

That same spring, my friend Luke went into the final phase of his life. We had met him and his mom during the Sadie's Sleigh Toy Shop at Children's Medical Center in Dallas. Afterward, he and I raced remote control cars all over the sixth floor.

And then Kelly. My nurse Kelly, the one who brought me toys and knew how to take away my pain and always said the right things, my nurse who knew what it was like because she had had cancer when she was a child: Kelly's baby boy was diagnosed with cancer.

I feel so much love for all of them, and so much anger. The anger drives me to do more. And the love: The love has to win.

There's hope that it will. The next chapter says how.

CHAPTER NINE

The Butterfly Effect

M any years ago, a scientist wrote, "Does the flap of a butterfly's wings in Brazil set off a tornado in Texas?"

Ever since then, people have talked about the Butterfly Effect. It's a real thing. People using computers to predict the future talk about it all the time. They use a complicated term for it: "Sensitive dependence on initial conditions." That means the tiniest change in the beginning can make humongous changes in the end. A butterfly's wings push the air, and that pushes a tiny amount of warm air in a different direction, and the warm air pushes against the cold air and things build up and make a storm front, and that causes a change in the upper atmosphere all the way to Texas, and, boom, tornado.

It's not just butterflies. It's people, too.

I first heard about the Butterfly Effect a few years ago, when we were doing an event for Sadie's Sleigh at a restaurant. A friend of my dad, Jamie Decker, gave a little speech. He told how when he was a senior in high school, his football coach and health teacher taught him and the other kids on his team how to do CPR and mouth-to-mouth resuscitation to save someone's life.

I don't need to know this, Mr. Jamie thought. *When would I ever use it?*

Mr. Jamie was coaching baseball for his summer job when he saw a kid get hit by a car while riding a bike. He ran over and the kid wasn't breathing. Jamie did CPR and breathed for the kid, keeping him alive until an ambulance came and took the kid away.

He didn't know what became of the boy until years later, when he was a grown man. He asked his mother whatever had happened to that boy.

"He's a children's oncologist now," she said.

Mr. Jamie thought, *I saved that kid's life so he could save other kids.* But then he told us in the restaurant, "I'm not the one who saved his life. Not really. It's the coach who saved his life, by teaching me CPR. But really, it's the person who taught the coach CPR, and the one who taught him, and so on down the line to the first person to teach CPR."

He was talking about the Butterfly Effect. Sensitive dependence on initial conditions. The world is sensitive to the beginning of things. And each of us, no matter how small and powerless, can be that beginning.

We're all butterflies. And when we do something small that leads to something big and changes the world for the better, then we begin to look a lot like angels.

The Butterfly Effect is all around me. When I first marched in the Rally to the Capitol with Tattoo Tom and hundreds of cancer fighters and supporters, my family and I seemed just like a few people, while together we were causing a tornado. But it all started even sooner than that, when I ducked into Mom's closet to record my first cancer video. I mean, I was just bored. It seemed like a fun thing to do to help people. It was like I was flapping tiny wings. And that video led to other videos and people shared them and Mr. Mike noticed them and made videos of me, and childhood cancer advocates noticed those videos and got Mr. Mike to introduce me to them, and they introduced me to Congressman McCaul, and he got me to lobby for the STAR Act.

And the STAR Act got passed by Congress and signed by the President of the United States. And kids' lives got saved.

It's not like my closet video *caused* everything to happen. It's just that, if I hadn't done that one little thing one night when I was bored, I wouldn't have been a part of all those big things. My own personal Butterfly Effect led to my own personal tornado, and I rode it. This was better than any roller coaster. (But then, I hate roller coasters.)

Even though many, many people worked hard to get the STAR Act passed, I got invited to the White House to watch the bill get signed into law. We heard from Congressman McCaul's office at four o'clock in the afternoon, the day before the signing. Did we want to go?

Yes, please!

"You need to be there by 11 o'clock."

Southwest Airlines had given us 20 vouchers to help us with our foundation and our advocacy. So Mom and I were able to fly from Dallas to Washington first thing the next morning. Our flight was at six a.m. I am barely alive before nine.

When we landed, we took a taxi to Congressman McCaul's house on Capitol Hill, where we changed clothes. Then we called an Uber to take us to his office.

I was freaking out. *Oh my gosh I'm going to meet the President today this is crazy!*

Congressman McCaul and I first met with reporters. By now I was used to that, so I said the things I usually say about being worth more than four percent and about my own Hard Time. We then went to the White House. When we went through the gate, we stopped for dogs to walk around the car and sniff for bombs or whatever. Then we got out and walked to security. It was like going through an airport, only the security people smiled more.

Then we walked into the West Wing. It's the most beautiful place, and it looks exactly the way it does on television. Aides took our cellphones and showed us into a room with couches and chairs, like a living room. Congressmen McCaul and other members of Congress were there, as well as two other former cancer fighters—teenagers named Olivia and Jake, along with their parents.

So were Danielle Leach and Kevin Mathis of St. Baldrick's. Ms. Danielle led this huge team to write the STAR Act and get it passed. St. Baldrick isn't really a saint. It's just a name that a few men in New York thought up: On St. Patrick's Day 20 years ago, they raised money by shaving heads in return for donations, $1,000 per head. In that first year they raised $17,000 to help pay for childhood cancer research. In the second year they raised $140,000. In the third year, a million! They've given well over a quarter of a billion dollars to childhood cancer science.

So why's it called St. Baldrick's? Because the big head-shaving events happen on St. Patrick's Day. Making people bald. Get it?

And that's why Danielle Leach of St. Baldrick's was in the room with me, waiting for the bill signing.

It seemed like everybody in that room knew who I was, even though I had never seen most of them in my life. Even the people who worked at the White House all knew about me.

A lady walked in. "We can come into the office now." Meaning the Oval Office. The President wasn't there. I looked around. Again, it looked exactly the way you think it does. One of the kids was standing next to the President's desk, and I stood next to him. One of the White House people said, "Can you and Sadie switch places? She's shorter."

"Yeah, sure." I figured it was for the pictures.

So now I was right next to the desk, with Mom behind me. I was so nervous. We waited forever, though it turned out to be just three minutes. People started walking in, then the door shut again. Each time, I thought it would be the President. Then seven more people walked in. *Not the President,* I figured. Only it was. He walked in last. It felt like I was watching TV, with the best, biggest screen you've ever seen. I was shaking a little.

He went around and shook everyone's hand. And then he reached down and shook mine. "How're you doin', Darling?"

He sat in his chair. I was right next to him, not sure what I was supposed to do. He took out some paper from a leather folder and said, "Let the press come in." An aide opened a door and a flood of cameras, seven boom mikes, and reporters rushed in. All I could hear was clicking, so loud I could barely hear anyone talking. Crazy.

The President said, "You see all these people?" He pointed to the reporters. "They are so nice. They love me. I get to do this every day."

I looked over at his desk and noticed that one of the papers had my name on it.

The President talked a bit about the STAR Act. Then he said, "We have three kids here today who helped pass the act." He talked about each one of us: Olivia, then Jake, then me. When he said "Sadie Keller," I thought: *A President just said my name!*

He asked Jake if he wanted to say anything. Jake said no. Then the President turned to me. "Do you want to say anything, darling?"

"Yes, I would," I said. "I'm just so honored to be here. This is just such an amazing opportunity, and, just, thank you."

Congressman McCaul talked, and then the President got ready to sign the bill. It was two pages long. Half of the second page was a bunch of words, and half was a big blank space where I supposed he would sign his name. He took out a big fat Sharpie marker pen. It has his own signature on it in gold. Taking off the cap, he signed his first name super fast, like he was scribbling. He turned to me. "Have you ever seen a signature like that?"

I laughed. "No."

He signed the rest of his name. All the pictures the press took show me laughing.

He showed off his signature, capped the marker and looked around. "Who should this pen go to?" He turned to me. "Here you go," and he handed it to me. I held it and was so nervous that I scraped it back and forth with my fingernail, scraping part of the President's name off the pen. But I actually have two pens, because he gave another one to Mom. I keep it in a shadow box. The pen he gave me has a big dent on the felt tip. That shows how hard he pushes down when he writes his name.

After he was done signing the bill, the press started yelling questions that had nothing to do with the bill. He answered one question, then his aides said, "Okay, okay" and pushed them out the door. We talked to more reporters in the White House and did an interview with NBC's Dallas station. That was a good day, which wouldn't have happened without that closet video. Butterfly Effect.

That new law, the STAR Act, led to all kinds of great childhood cancer research. And earlier legislation that Congressman McCaul worked on helped lead to new exciting treatments. Which started from a very different butterfly.

Way back in 1965, Jim Allison was a student at the University of Texas. His dad was a country doctor in Alice,

Texas, where Jim grew up. Jim figured he would become a doctor, too, so he was majoring in premed, studying so he could get into medical school. But the more he studied, the more interested he became in what science *didn't* know about the human body. So he switched majors and ended up getting a Ph.D. in biochemistry and became really interested in the new science of the immune system, which is all the things in your body that attack disease.

Along the way he found himself focusing on cancer. His mother had died of it; he had held her hand as she passed. And he had lost many others in his family to cancer. His research on the immune system led him to believe it might be a big answer to cancer.

The main immune attackers are called T cells. The biggest of these are hunters and killers. They go after anything foreign in your body, like viruses and bacteria, the things that give you colds and infections. When these giant T cells find these foreign invaders, they grab them and swallow them up. Meanwhile, these hunters just hang out. They don't attack anything until they find something foreign.

Now the question was: How do these T cells figure out what's foreign and what isn't? Nobody knew. But if scientists could find out, maybe they could find a way to send the T cells to attack cancer. Maybe the T cells could be like bloodhounds. *Here, T cell! Here, doggie! Sniff this sock* (only not a sock but a protein called an antigen). *Now, go get 'em!*

Except that a dog has a nose. A T cell has...what? The T cell version of a nose must be some kind of receptor— a detector that can sniff what's foreign.

Jim Allison read all the research he could, attended the lectures of leading scientists and came up with a way to, well, detect the detector. At the time, he was pretty much a nobody. He hadn't discovered anything important yet. But his research was proven right. And it changed the way scientists thought about the immune system.

The thing about science, though, is that an answer just leads to more questions. So Dr. Allison found the receptor (yay!). Other scientists did experiments showing how the receptor clicked onto the foreign protein. But when the receptor did that in the laboratory, the T cell...did nothing. It just hung around. Something had to turn it on. After a while, Dr. Allison found a chemical that did just that. But the T cell got going and then...stopped. Scientists found another T cell protein they thought might be a second gas pedal.

Except that Dr. Allison realized that wasn't exactly it. He thought, *Maybe it isn't a gas pedal. Maybe it's a brake.* It didn't turn the T cell on. It turned the cell off.

And everybody was like, holy cow. So this is how the T cell works. It finds a foreign protein, an antigen. That lights up the T cell. Another chemical signal fires it up and makes it go. Then another chemical hits the brakes. Why? Because otherwise the T cell might go crazy and start attacking good things in the body it doesn't recognize, causing an autoimmune disease like lupus or even going after a newly conceived baby inside a mother's womb.

Somehow, cancer was making the T cell hit the brakes. What would happen if Dr. Allison took those brakes off when the cell recognized cancer? He invented a drug that took off the brakes.

It worked. And it led to scientists understanding the immune system in a whole new way. That knowledge led to a new type of treatment called immune checkpoint blockade that's used to treat 16 different types of cancer, and counting.

All this started after Jim Allison decided to switch majors in college in 1965. He won the Nobel Prize for Medicine in 2018. Even better, the new treatment is curing kids, and more treatments are coming. It's still really, really new, though. The treatments don't always work, and we're still losing children to cancer. And that's why it's so important that we have laws to encourage drug companies and scientists to keep working on more ways to fight childhood cancer.

Meanwhile, other scientists are finding ways to help the immune system fight cancer. In the 1980s, they began trying to change the genes of T cells. One scientist in Israel made a discovery that became an amazing therapy called CAR-T. The T is for T cell. The CAR stands for, wait for it: Chimeric Antigen Receptor. "Chimeric" means something made from parts of different things. It comes from the chimera, a creature from old-time tales that was a lion with the head of a goat and a snake's tail. In medicine, a chimeric protein combines two different genes. A chimeric antigen receptor takes the genes from a virus and sticks them into a T cell. The genes cause the T cell to make receptors that can spot a foreign protein, or antigen, on a cancer tumor. The scientist in Israel discovered the first chimeric antigen receptor. It works for a cancer fighter, such as a kid with leukemia, this way:

Blood gets taken out of the kid's body. Then the white cells, including T cells, get separated from the rest of the blood, and the blood—minus the white cells—get put back into the kid. The hospital sends the T cells to a laboratory, which puts in a virus that carries genes that make the T cells attack just the right cancer cells. The lab then grows millions of these T cells, and the virus spreads the genes. They're then put back into the kid. The cells attack the cancer.

The even cooler thing is, the cells then hang around after the cancer is gone. The genes make the cells remember the cancer and attack any cancer cells that come out of hiding.

Honestly, I don't completely understand all of this. My brother, Grant, can explain it better. The important thing is, in 2017, the FDA approved the first CAR-T treatment for children and young adults with my kind of leukemia, and experiments are being done on treatments for other kinds of cancer—thanks in part to the new childhood cancer laws being passed.

Which leads me to another butterfly, Congressman McCaul, though you wouldn't think he was a butterfly if you met him. Even before the scientists were coming up with the big breakthroughs, the Congressman realized he needed more high-powered help. He thought, *Why not form a caucus?* This is what helped lead to all those great new childhood cancer laws.

That's when members of Congress get together around an interest. There's an animal protection caucus, a mental health caucus, a zoo and aquarium caucus (I would join that one!), medical caucuses for different adult diseases, and many, many others. There's even a cement caucus! Congressman McCaul thought, *Why not a childhood cancer caucus?* So he started one with Congressman Chris Van Hollen of Maryland. There are now lots of members of Congress in the caucus, including Democrats and Republicans, men and women. I get to meet pretty often with some of the other co-chairs, including Jackie Speier, Mike Kelly, and G. K. Butterfield. They're all the nicest people to me. Talking to one or the other, you wouldn't know their politics. They're all passionate about the cause of stopping the biggest killer of small children by disease.

So:

Dad's friend Mr. Jamie saved a little boy through CPR, thanks to a butterfly who taught someone CPR, who taught someone else CPR, and so on until Mr. Jamie's coach learned CPR and taught Mr. Jamie, who saved the boy, who became a childhood cancer doctor saving the lives of children. And that first butterfly became the best of angels.

A student at the University of Texas, Jim Allison, got curious about how the immune system worked, and then discovered how killer T cells get turned on and off, and that led to more discoveries, which led to using kids' own immune systems to save their lives.

I know one of those kids who were saved. And that makes Dr. Jim Allison a butterfly who became an angel.

Then there's me. I got bored and made a closet video and made a jillion friends who bought presents to bring to kids, and other friends who were activists let me join them to help get laws passed, and those laws helped scientists do research on new treatments like Dr. Allison's and CAR-T, and those treatments saved children.

Which, not to brag or anything, makes me the luckiest butterfly of all. But I'm not done. I'm not nearly done.

CHAPTER TEN

The Hard Time Becomes the Giving Time

don't mean to make you think any of this is easy. None of it is easy—not the treatment, or getting bills passed in Congress, or, most of all, the facts about childhood cancer. This is a fight, and fights are hard.

So here are the facts:

Most kids with cancer get leukemia or brain cancer. A third of these kids get leukemia. That's what I had. Nobody knows why kids get cancer. Nobody knows the causes...yet.

More than 15,000 kids get diagnosed with cancer every year. Seven kids die every day. The number is growing, too. Again, nobody knows why. Yet.

The good news is, a kid with cancer has a much, much better chance of surviving these days. Before my parents were born, back in the 1970s, almost half of kids diagnosed with cancer died. These days, kids have an eight in ten chance of surviving five years after treatment. That's because the treatments have gotten a whole lot better. But they still need to get even better so that cancer stops being the number one killer of children by disease. And in order for the treatment to get better, scientists have to find out more about what causes cancer in kids.

This is why scientists are some of the most humble people on earth. Most people are proud of what they know. I'm proud of all I've learned about cancer and treatments and how a bill gets passed in Congress. But scientists get excited more by what they *don't* know.

What weird things are going on with the
immune system?
Scientists: We don't know, exactly.

Why don't cancer cells know how to die?
Why do some cells forget that part of the code,
while others don't?
Scientists: We can't wait to learn that.

How do T cells remember foreign invaders?
Scientists: We've learned a lot about that!
But, um, we don't know exactly how they do it.

Why doesn't CAR-T treatment work all the time
on kids with cancer?
Scientists: We're working very, very hard to
find out.

It doesn't get more humble than that. Scientists are the exact opposite of know-it-alls. They see knowledge the way I see a blank sheet of paper when I want to do art. We both want to fill in the blank spaces. The blank space for scientists is ignorance—the knowledge they admit they don't have. Which is humble. And also hopeful.

Another kind of blank space is people's need to know more about a cause like ours. To fill that space, I have tried to get better at telling our story. For some reason,

I've always found it easier to talk in front of a camera. It's less crowded. It's more like talking to a few friends.

I love doing sleepovers with my friends. A year ago, a friend had a sleepover for her birthday party. I knew all the girls who were there. All the time I had known them, they had never asked about my cancer.

This one night, though, we were trying to pick a movie to watch. Instead, all the kids started asking me questions about my cancer and my foundation and all I had been through. Which was weird: We had been trying to pick a movie. But it was like they had all been thinking about my cancer; they just didn't know how to ask. Even then, some of them seemed embarrassed, like they didn't want to hurt my feelings.

"You can ask me anything," I said. "Every question is a great question."

That opened the gates, like, big time.

"What did you go through during your chemo?"

"What was it like when you were diagnosed?"

"Did you have to get poked?"

"Did it hurt to get chemo?"

"What do you do with your foundation?"

"Will one of us ever get cancer?"

This last question was a big one. Seeing a kid who has had cancer makes other kids think more about getting it.

"You never really know," I said. "But I pretty much know that none of y'all are ever going to get it. And if you do, I'll be here for you and you can get through it."

I can talk just fine with my friends. But when I meet a new person without my mom or dad or brother, I'm super awkward. I don't know what to say. This is why it might seem weird that I can talk to strangers in front of a camera. But people need to know about childhood cancer, so I kind of flip a switch.

Besides, Mom's almost always there. And lots of times, Congressman McCaul is with me, especially when we're talking about bills before Congress. And a lot of the people who have interviewed me are my friends now.

Maybe it's the camera itself. I can't see the thousands or millions of people on the other end. At any rate, I've done more than 50 television interviews. Practice makes—well, not perfect. Better.

It started right after I did the first closet video, in September of 2015. My hospital reached out to Mom. "It's Childhood Cancer Awareness month," the public relations person said. She asked if she could pitch one of my closet videos.

I said okay, and the next day Mom and I met Katy Blakey of Dallas's NBC station at the hospital. I wore a red dress that reminded me of the dress Annie wears in "Little Orphan Annie," along with a leopard print scarf on my head. There's a picture of me with Miss Katy from that day. I had just finished the hardest phase of my treatment—Delayed Intensification or DI, when you get packed with chemo. My face was chipmunk-y. Because I had no hair, my forehead was more like a seventeenhead.

And I not only had no hair, I had no eyebrows or lashes. Plus, I was really thin from all the chemo.

But Katy talked to us in the kindest way. She asked how I made that video. And she asked me about the treats I was taking to the nurses and doctors every week. "What made you start taking things to them?"

"They just do so much for me that I thought I should just give a little something to them," I squeaked. My voice was tiny back then.

Katy also interviewed Caitlin, my child life specialist, along with my nurse practitioner, Maria. When Katy asked Caitlin what it meant to her that I was doing those things, Caitlin said, "Our hope is always for a child to have a positive attitude, and Sadie is really special about it." And then Caitlin cried.

Over the next months and years, we learned how hard it can be for people who work on the childhood cancer floor. Some of the kids really struggle, crying all the time and getting sicker and sicker. And the nurses and doctors do all they can to be cheerful even when they want to cry. One of my favorite nurses at clinic, Kelly Brown, the one who'd had childhood cancer (chondrosarcoma, a kind of bone cancer), was always positive and fun, always had a smile on her face.

When my treatment was winding down and we started going in less often, Kelly had a beautiful baby boy named Lucas. When he was just a few months old, he was diagnosed with a rhabdoid tumor, a cancer of the kidney.

Several months later, Lucas passed away. I was shocked, and we were so sad.

Think about it: Kelly went from being a childhood cancer patient to dedicating her life to helping kids with cancer to losing her baby to cancer. We were all family, the nurses and kids and parents, but the nurses and doctors on the sixth floor were like an even closer family. And they really struggled with what happened. Some of them ended up transferring to other parts of the hospital. Others just left. I don't blame them. Their hearts were broken.

It's a story that's hard to hear, and it's really hard to tell. But the stories have to be told. We all need to hear them so that we can understand how important the childhood cancer-fighting laws and science and medicine are—and why we all have to do something to change the story. I can afford to be positive, because I've been incredibly lucky. But I never stop thinking about the kids, and mothers and fathers and sisters and brothers, who have not been so fortunate.

Katy Blakey did another interview with me a couple months later, when we were gearing up for Sadie's Sleigh. Since then we've done maybe 20 more interviews. And she's the MC at my Sadie Keller Foundation events.

Two years ago, after I had started lobbying Congress, I had my first national interview. Congressman McCaul brought me to New York for a media tour. First was Arthel Neville for a Fox News Sunday show. We met her before we went in front of the cameras, and she seemed really nice. But now I was nervous. This was going to be live! What if I messed up right on live national television?

We went into the studio five minutes before the start, while they were on commercial break. We sat at a big table with four or five cameras around. The lights are brighter than they seem on TV. The director person said "One minute!" Then, "Thirty seconds!" Then he counted down from ten like a rocket launch, and we were on. Miss Arthel started reading from her paper, talking about "the little girl and the congressman on their mission to fight childhood cancer." She turned and said hi to me even before she thanked the Congressman for being there, which I thought was funny. Then she said, "I've already fallen in love with Sadie, so Congressman, pardon me if I push you to the side for a moment, no disrespect."

Congressman McCaul laughed. Then Miss Arthel and I talked about Sadie's Sleigh. At the end, she asked me how being a cancer survivor "changed my outlook on life."

Outlook? What does that mean? I had no idea. I paused to think of an answer. It seemed like I was just sitting there staring for five seconds. But when I watched the video afterward, I saw that I didn't pause at all. "Well, I feel like—like knowing about childhood cancer makes you like a better person." Then I just said what I want to say. "I just want to point out that kids get cancer, too. I'm a big advocate for children with cancer. They only get four percent of funding from the government."

Experts on being interviewed say you should answer the question you wished they asked, not the one they actually ask. So you could say I was really smart to answer the way I did. But honestly, I just didn't know what "outlook" meant.

Miss Arthel tweeted after the show, "Sadie Keller is my new hero/#shero..."

Next day we did another news program, and then another live interview, this time on "Varney & Company," which was weird because that's a financial show.

But the big deal came a month later, when CBS's "Inside Edition" came to our house. They shot our photo party for Sadie's Sleigh and interviewed me. That segment has gotten more than a million views online. Half of those views are probably mine. I watch it over and over because it's so cool to see my house and our cul-de-sac and friends and all those tons of presents. Plus the comments people make on the website have been great. Which doesn't always happen online.

Another big appearance was when CNN's Wolf Blitzer interviewed Congressman McCaul and me, right after the signing of the STAR Act. When we were ready to go home that day, we changed clothes and headed to the airport, and as we were walking in, a lady stopped me and said, "Did I just see you on TV?" CNN was playing all over the TVs in the airport.

I don't remember what I said in that one. In interviews, I just sort of focus and then the rest of my mind blacks out.

I've gotten better at speaking since the first closet video I did when I was seven. Practice helps. And it's nice to have hair again, though I never was really bothered by being bald when I did the closet videos. I thought more about helping other kids than I did about what I looked like, and that made me less self-conscious, I guess. Besides, I love to do all of the television to raise awareness for childhood cancer. Even if we're talking about Sadie's Sleigh, we're still talking about childhood cancer. When I think about being the voice for other kids, it's not like I'm the one on television. I'm a voice.

Which, when I think about it, is a pretty good tip. To feel less embarrassed, don't think about yourself. Think about others.

And other people are doing the same. During our second year of Sadie's Sleigh, the Boy Scouts did a toy drive for us. Their national headquarters is in Dallas, and I spoke there. While I was on stage, the lady opened this humongous box, the biggest you ever saw—five of me, maybe ten, could fit in there. She had several people pull out a giant bear. "Sadie, Merry Christmas!" We have this little nook in our game room. We put the bear in the corner with my bookshelf and stuffed animals, and now it's a reading area. I sit in it and read, and Louie likes to hide in there and sleep.

After I finished my chemo treatment, I got to actually be with the kids when they got their Christmas presents. Before that, while I was still getting treatment, I wasn't allowed access to the kids. We could make each other sick because of our compromised immune systems. So when I finally got permission, we decided to go big with it. Instead of just delivering the toys to kids' rooms, we opened a Sadie's Sleigh Toy Shop in the hospital's family room on the sixth floor, the cancer floor. We did it a few days before Christmas so that even the kids who were able to go home for the holiday could still get presents.

The morning of the Toy Shop was the same morning the moving trucks came to pick up all the presents from our house. We had the toys all packed up in gigantic boxes. Ten grownups could fit in just one of them. The boxes were organized by types: girl, boy, baby, teenager, that sort of thing. One of the boxes was just for the Toy Shop. It contained some of the biggest, best toys. We followed the two trucks to Children's. Some two dozen Child Life specialists and volunteers were waiting for us at the front of the hospital. They had big laundry bins to put the presents in. As we pulled up, they whooped and hollered and ran toward the trucks. The movers unloaded the toys, and the Child Life people stuffed their laundry bins and rolled them to be stored for Christmas Day. We had a couple bins for the Toy Shop, and we took them up to the sixth floor. There were ten of us, half with the Sadie Keller Foundation (including Mom and me) and half Child Life people, all there to organize the Toy Shop.

The family room isn't that big, but we arranged more than a thousand toys in there. The place was packed when we were done. Toys on chairs and tables, toys on the floor, toys high, toys low. There were Nerf guns, baby dolls, video games, American Girl dolls, JBL speakers for the teenagers, Polaroid cameras, remote control trucks and cars, big Barbie sets, a 2,000-piece Lego set, Amazon Fire tablets, trucks and cars you could ride on around the hospital, even a small claw machine. I loved it. It was like a magic toy explosion.

That morning, Child Life and the nurses had passed out postcards announcing the Toy Shop, so patients were ready. They started streaming in as soon as we were done setting up. Kids came in with their IV poles—some with their moms, some with their sisters and brothers. The teenagers mostly came by themselves. Some parents came without their kids, who were on isolation and had to stay in their rooms. Everyone's reaction was like the happiest thing you have ever seen in your life. I wish you could see it: kids getting the toys they always wanted. You know how you go into a toy store and say, "Mom, I want that!" and Mom usually says no? On that wonderful day, Sadie's Sleigh Toy Shop Day, it was all yes.

But it wasn't just one toy. Each kid got to pick out three toys. Some of the kids were overwhelmed. I helped them, asking what they liked and showing them toys they missed. Then we helped carry the toys back to their rooms. The brothers and sisters got toys, too. Some parents asked if they could take toys for siblings who couldn't be there. "Absolutely!" we said. "What do they like?"

One of the best parts came after, when the kids and their parents hugged me. Some of the parents told me that seeing me do all this and look so happy and healthy gives them hope for their own kids: "Seeing you so well and doing all this for us makes us believe we're going to get through this, too."

And after everybody had gone, we still had plenty of toys left over to add to Sadie's Sleigh.

We did the Toy Shop again the next year and the next, and we're excited to start other hospitals too. And Sadie's Sleigh keeps growing and growing. Last year at Children's, we donated more than 7,000 toys, so many that some of those were left over on Christmas Day. The hospital stored them, and gave some on kids' birthdays or when they finished chemo or had a hard time. I know how it feels to get a toy at a time like that. I'll never forget how much an American Girl doll cheered me up the first month I was in the hospital.

Still, we thought it wasn't enough to help just the kids. Childhood cancer is hard on the parents, too. Besides the fear and the sadness and the agony of seeing your child in pain, there's a terrible drain on family finances and time. No matter how good your medical insurance is, families face the cost of all kinds of other things: all the meals they have to eat out because they're not home, the gas for driving back and forth to the hospital a couple times a week, the runs to Walmart or Target for stuff they never needed before their kid ended up in the hospital.

So we started giving out bags with a Visa gift card, a blanket, and snacks. Now we give out what we call Parent Packs. The parent gets a notebook with a calendar, and a cellphone sleeve so the parent can put gift cards and credit cards right with their phone. This was Mom's idea. (Honestly, the whole Parent Pack was my parents' idea.) It happens a lot: The parent steps out of the kid's hospital room to make a call, then while she's out of the room she runs down to buy a cup of coffee, then realizes she doesn't have her wallet. And once a parent leaves the room, it's hard on the kid to have her just come and go again. That's what the cellphone sleeve is for.

And with each Parent Pack are five gift cards worth $100 apiece: Uber Eats or Door Dash, Walmart, Target, gas cards, that sort of thing. Plus an Amazon card. The food delivery cards are perfect for when the kid (like me) refuses to eat any more of the hospital food, when she's on steroids making her hangry. And with the shopping cards, the parents can have stuff delivered right to the hospital.

Nothing in the Parent Pack is wasted. Parents in the hospital will get a ton of folders and binders, and they usually end up never using them. Mom wanted to make sure that every single piece was helpful.

You should meet Mom sometime. She's really kind of a genius with things like that.

Each month, social workers give the Parent Packs to people who need them. And then on Christmas we give a pack to every cancer kid family. We hope to give more and more of them. We buy everything for the packs ourselves, through the foundation. Someday we hope to have businesses donate the gift cards. But meanwhile, we raise the money ourselves.

Our biggest fundraising event is the Yellow Ball. The yellow means smiles—happy, positive, all the things I try to be. We have the event every September—Childhood Cancer Awareness Month, and just before we start gearing up for Sadie's Sleigh. For this last one, 400 people showed up. They can buy a single ticket or a whole table. All kinds of people come—Dallas people, supporters from all over, friends, people who followed my story, people I don't even know. Two couples from season 15 of "The Bachelor" even came, including Mike and Connor S. Important businesspeople like Bill Hutchinson and Mehrdad Moayedi also came.

We held it in the Jet Ten airplane hangar at the airport in Addison. Everyone wore yellow. We had two acrobats hanging from ribbons attached way up in the ceiling. There was a Step and Repeat, like what actors pose in front of at the Oscars. I took a lot of pictures with people. And we had this amazing magician. He marked an X on his hand with a Sharpie and made it disappear off his skin. Then he asked my Aunt Erica to make two fists. "Open them," he said. And there was an X on her own hand! There were singers and a band, and a VIP party in a smaller area before it all started.

The food was donated: I had chicken wrapped in bacon with mashed potatoes. Far better than hospital food.

Katy Blakey MC'd, and I spoke. I use notes I put on my iPhone, with the order of things I'll say and people's names in case I forget. I talked about the families of cancer fighters. "It's like the whole family is diagnosed," I said.

And I talked about the need for legislation and more research. I did fine, I think. But every time I finish speaking and go offstage I think, *I hope I can do that again.*

We honored six childhood cancer fighters that day—two teenagers, a few four- and five-year-olds, and a girl my age. I called each one onstage to give them the Sadie's Fighter Award. The award is beautiful: an acrylic and glass teardrop with a gold ribbon on it. Each of their parents got a Parent Pack with $500 in gift cards and a check for $1,000.

After that I gave a Sadie's Hero Award to an 11-year-old boy who raised money for my foundation. Christian Weeresinghe didn't have cancer, but he heard my story at Covenant Church in Dallas. The church had invited me to come and tell it during Sunday service. Christian was there, and the story inspired him. He wrote letters to people and got help from friends. I didn't even know he was doing this. Then after school one day, Mom said, "We have to go to the church. You have a little interview to do." When I walked in, Christian was sitting there. He explained that he had already raised $16,000.

I was shocked. "Oh my gosh, thank you so much!"

"I'm not done," he said. "My goal is $25,000."

A few weeks later, he met that goal. Twenty-five thousand dollars. My family and his family ate lunch after church one day, and he gave me the money. So we wanted to give him a special award for doing that.

And we go to Covenant Church every Sunday now.

You know how I told you about scientists filling in the blank spaces of cancer knowledge? And how I try to fill in the blank spaces about cancer in people's minds? The biggest blank spaces have to do with the laws that still need passing. That's why the Childhood Cancer Summit is so important. And CureFest.

I've been to four CureFests now. More and more people show up every year—over 3,000 this last time. But it still seems like a big family reunion. I speak each year, and my family and I still march in the front with Tattoo Tom. He has this club, and my friend Lily and I got inducted into it. He calls it the Two Feathers Society. It's an honor. He gives you a beautiful ring with two feathers on it. I'm not allowed to tell you what they mean. Tattoo Tom says, "You must never share the secret of the ring." So I can't share that. I wear the ring on my right pointer finger. It's the finger that fits the best; I love that ring!

My friend Lily looked really good last year. We had been friends four years at that point, but I felt like I knew her my whole life. In the summer of 2018, she and I spoke together. Lily talked about her relapse and the Trading Places picture Mr. Mike had taken of us, which had now gone viral. "Now we both stand up here cancer free!" she said. We high-fived. And everybody cheered really loud.

I also saw my friend Tatum. I hadn't seen her in three or four years. The last time I had seen her, we went to Party City with Mr. Mike and made a video with wigs. She wore a lot of wigs, even though I didn't. She had Ewing's sarcoma and had to have a bone marrow transplant, going through a really hard time. This was the first time she was well enough to come to CureFest. We hugged for a long time and she started crying. You can't meet people like that in normal life.

Then there was this sweet five-year-old girl who came up to us. Her family was waiting for us. We were walking over to Freedom Plaza, and a mom stopped us and said, "Sadie? My daughter is a huge fan of yours. She's watched all your videos. She keeps telling me she wants to start a foundation like Sadie."

Her name was Summer, and she had leukemia. She hugged me. She had curly short hair. As we were leaving, she said, sounding a little shy, "You can come over to my house if you want."

Kids who have gotten Milestone Gifts also came up to us. One of them was about Summer's age. She wore face paint and a Wonder Woman crown. Her name was Brixton. She had rhabdomyosarcoma, and her mom let us know that she had just relapsed and would be starting chemo again.

A few months later, just when we were finishing this book, we got the most terrible news. It was just before Christmas, and Mom and I were doing some shopping. We had just delivered the Sadie's Sleigh toys in Dallas. It was a big year for us: a total of 22,500 toys for children who have to spend Christmas in the hospital. The work of Sadie's Sleigh had kept us from shopping for our own family, so we were doing that. We stopped to have lunch and to celebrate. And that's when Mom got the news. She got a text and looked upset but wouldn't tell me what it was.

We finished lunch and sat in the car for what seemed like 15 minutes. I stared at my phone. Finally, I asked. "Mom? What was on your phone?" I had a feeling that something horrible had happened.

She didn't say anything for a whole minute. She just sat there, staring through the windshield.

I felt my heart beating through my chest and into my neck. I was shaking.

Mom turned to me. "I just found out: Lily has passed away."

I put my hand over my mouth. "What?" Not Lily. Oh, not wonderful, smiling, joyful, best friend Lily. We knew she had taken a turn, had relapsed. We knew she had been on chemo again. We all knew it wasn't good, but we hadn't heard any news. The family had come together in the end, just being together.

I searched my brain for something to say. "I'm really anxious," I said. "I mean I don't know what I'm supposed to do."

We kept sitting there in the car, talking about Lily. "She has been fighting since she was ten," Mom said. "She's visiting Ariella in Heaven." Ariella was one of our friends who passed away, and she and Lily were close.

I nodded, and Mom started the car. I checked Facebook and Instagram on my phone. People were already posting a picture of Lily and Ariella reunited in Heaven. Now we didn't have to worry about more bad news for Lily. Her family didn't have to worry anymore.

"But it's so hard," I said. "I don't understand. How could this happen if we were all praying so hard? Why didn't God heal her?"

"We can't know," Mom said. "But think of the life Lily led. Think of the thousands of lives she touched."

I sniffed. "Millions. And now she's in Heaven and not in pain."

A few days later, we flew back to D.C. and went to her service in Maryland. I saw some friends who were cancer fighters. Lily would have loved to see them, too, and the service was just the way she would have wanted it.

But honestly, I still can't understand why Lily's life ended so soon. She had only graduated from high school a few months before, and she'd hoped to go to college.

But.

Lily *lived*. She lived *a lot*. Some people might live a hundred years and not have as many smiles as Lily had in 18. Some people might live lives that aren't as much living—being an advocate, speaking out for childhood cancer, being the best kind of friend—as Lily lived.

Maybe this is the real story. Most of us measure our lives in years. When we get sick—from cancer, from whatever—doctors and nurses do all they can to give us more years. I want more years, all I can get. But that's not the only measure of a life. How much you live isn't all about the years, but about the people you touch, the difference you make, and the joy you bring to others.

My heart hurts for Lily and her family. It literally hurts. But I believe she lived more, did more, than many people who live much longer.

When Lily was still in remission, before the cancer came back, she wrote about how she was diagnosed with cancer when she was in fifth grade. "If I could go back in time and be a ten-year-old with a clean bill of health, I wouldn't. This is my fight. For me, this fight will never be over. We will always be fighting for more funding and fighting for a cure. This fight will be with me forever, and I wouldn't want it any other way."

Here on Earth, we're still fighting. Lily and Tatum and Summer and Sadie Murata and Brixton and so many others are why Mom and I do what we do. And they're why Congressman McCaul and the Childhood Cancer Caucus do what they do. In honor of Lily, I'm trying to fight with a smile.

She and all my friends in the fight are why I feel so incredibly lucky, luckier than if I had never been diagnosed in the first place. Still, if you've never been diagnosed, I hope you won't. Chances are you won't. But I hope you can see what I learned from all of this.

Because we all go through Hard Times. Some of us, many Hard Times. The question isn't whether we will. It's how we deal with it—how we *live*. It's about taking on the fight, and then going on to fight for others. It's about being willing to help, and give, and even march when we have to, even if we're not the marching type. It's about letting people like Christian and the members of Congress and all the people hear your story and take action. It's about letting all the helpers and the comforters and the true friends into your life, even when you know you may lose some of them to Heaven.

It's about welcoming all the better angels.

Love,

Sadie

How to Change the World

*The people dwelling in darkness
have seen a great light,
and for those dwelling in the region
  and shadow of death,
on them a light has dawned.*

Matthew 4:16

Tragedy makes angels. It's a fact of life that makes us human. Sadie and I have both lost friends to childhood cancer. And we have made new ones who have survived cancer—along with many more friends who have stepped up to make it so that more and more survive.

My own childhood cancer quest began many years ago, when I was in fourth grade. I grew up in the University Park neighborhood of Dallas and went to Christ the King, a Catholic grade school. One of my best friends at that school, Todd Tenholder, was a neighbor. He was a good student, and everybody liked him. Some kids could be mean—there wasn't a lot of adult supervision back then—but Todd was a sweet kid. He'd join the rest of us kids in playing games in the street: Kick the Can, baseball, hot potato, that sort of thing.

I'd ride my bicycle over to his house, and he would join me riding through the many parks in that neighborhood. Kids roamed free back then, and we'd run through the

155

woods like wildlife. There was a drainage system with big concrete pipes and culverts, and we'd crawl through them pretending we were amateur detectives like the Hardy Boys, ending up at the lake the pipes emptied into. In summertime we would play until ten o'clock, when our parents said we had to be home. Then we'd sleep at one or the other's house, talking into the night.

One day, when school was in session, I noticed that Todd looked different. His sandy hair looked thin, with bald patches. He seemed pale. "Hey, Todd," I said, "are you okay?"

He shook his head. "I'm sick."

I only learned later that he had leukemia. Back then it was a death sentence, and over the following weeks, he got worse and worse. The next thing I knew, I was going to his funeral. I was nine years old and couldn't understand what had happened. But I knew I had lost the best friend a kid could have.

Even before I got elected to Congress, a couple talked to me about the need to do something about childhood cancer. Tim and Donna Culliver had lost their son, Adam, to cancer. They were trying to get members of Congress interested in doing something about the disease. Not many were paying attention back then, a decade ago. "We want you to join us," they said.

I thought of my friend Todd. It was an easy decision. "Sure," I said. "Of course."

Back then, the people passionate about childhood

cancer didn't have much of a voice. They were voiceless and powerless. But they were persistent, and I was able to help them.

After I was elected, they handed me a bat signed by kids who had fought cancer. Some of them survived; some of them aren't alive today. The bat said TAKE A SWING AT CHILDHOOD CANCER. I picked up that bat and decided to form a caucus—a group of members of Congress who gather around a cause.

This is how you change the world. You get passionate about something that needs change; then you find people who are equally passionate. You join forces, gather people, and give a voice to the voiceless.

Many of the advocates are parents of kids who had cancer. Some of the kids made it, and some didn't. In each case the family is turning a bad situation into a positive one. They tell me many sad stories that are hard to hear. I'm the father of five children, and I simply can't imagine losing one of them. Yet it happens all the time— an average of seven children each day. Fifteen thousand kids in the United States were diagnosed with cancer in the last year alone. Cancer is the number one disease killing our children.

I have a stack of cards with pictures of the advocates' kids. You can't help but be moved by them. But all of the parents and survivors are doing more than telling hard stories; their message is one of hope, a vision for the future where they can make a difference. They want to make sure their children didn't die in vain. These advocates have learned to turn suffering into meaning—a lesson my father taught me. He was my hero. He served as a bombardier on a B-17, participated in the D-Day air campaign during World War II, and died from cancer when I was very young. An experience like losing a loved one is *cathartic*. That's a word I often use in talking about childhood cancer and the way people deal with it. A catharsis purifies the soul by taking you through extremes of fear and pain, or by making you feel great pity for others. It's a healing process—one that heals us all.

But not in the beginning. Not 15 years ago, when the Cullivers first approached me. Back then, the only type of treatments for kids with cancer were radiation, invasive surgery, and—mostly—chemotherapy, these brutally high doses of chemicals. As Sadie puts it, chemo is poison. You hope it kills the cancer cells before the poison kills you.

Chemo's history with cancer started during World War II, when some of the doctors began injecting cancer patients with mustard gas (sulfur mustard and nitrogen mustard). This poison gas had killed or crippled thousands of soldiers in World War I. You may have seen pictures of soldiers wearing gas masks. They were trying to protect themselves from mustard gas. The researchers started looking into all the effects of the gas on humans; some of them became cancer doctors, and they began experimenting by injecting sulfur mustard and nitrogen mustard directly into adult cancer patients. A few of the patients got better for a while, but most patients got worse—in part because of the poison itself. Still, the notion of using poison to kill cancer caught on and became the main type of cancer therapy to this day. Believe it or not, a few cancer drugs still use chemicals made from mustard agents. (None of them were used on Sadie, thank goodness.)

In the past decade, though, scientists began to learn more and more about how cells work. They studied the immune system and found ways to manipulate the genes that help tell cells what to do. Advances were made in new treatments. All except for a tiny bit of that research was devoted to adults with cancer.

Back then, Congress wasn't doing much for childhood cancer, either. Only one of my colleagues was paying attention: Deborah Pryce, a Representative from Ohio. Her daughter had died of cancer. In 2008, she and I got a bill passed to advance medical research and treatments for childhood cancer. The President signed it, but it got barely funded. This is pretty common: Congress decides to do something, and it passes a law, but paying for it requires separate legislation—and a whole lot of patience.

At first, Congress was an echo chamber. Tim and Donna Culliver would lobby members and they would say, "Why should I do anything about this?" Here they were talking about the number one killer of children by disease. Over the years, though, the numbers of advocates grew, and so did the members of the Childhood Cancer Caucus.

Why do we need a separate caucus for cancer that affects kids? To give them a voice in Congress. As Sadie likes to say, children are our future. While research on adult cancer is important, look at the difference between the potential life years lost when we lose a child to cancer, as opposed to an adult. When an adult dies of cancer, we lose 15 potential life years. When a kid dies of cancer, we lose 70 potential life years. It's a terrible loss. But kids have more future potential. When we save a kid, we save potential—the opportunity to invent the next big technology, to lead the nation, to solve diseases, to create the future.

Yet kids with cancer get fewer kinds of treatment. Hundreds of modern treatments have been approved by the federal government for cancer, with just three developed specifically for children. What's more, childhood cancer research gets only a small fraction of the total American cancer-research budget.

Remember: One in 285 children will get diagnosed with cancer this year. Every day, doctors diagnose 43 children with cancer. That's like an entire schoolroom. Forty-three sets of parents hear the horrible news. Forty-three kids suddenly find themselves having to go through the scary procedures—the shots, the operations, the ports in the chest, everything Sadie described and sometimes more. The average age at diagnosis is three to five years. So the typical childhood cancer patient hasn't even started kindergarten yet.

This just breaks your heart, doesn't it? How can we ignore something like that?

The good news is, we're not ignoring it. I've been teaming up with kids and adults to change how kids with cancer get treated—while giving scientists what they need to come up with new kinds of cancer-fighting medicines. Sadie is one of those teammates. So is the woman who introduced me to Sadie. Her name is Nancy Goodman, and you really want to meet her.

Nancy's son, Jacob, was a normal, healthy eight-year-old boy when they got the news that he was sick with medulloblastoma, a kind of brain cancer. Jacob went through nine months of hospital treatment, including two stem cell transplants, which gave him terrible pain. He was in a wheelchair. His brain gave him trouble with words and problems with tracking things with his eyes. Through much of the treatment, he couldn't read. Two years after his diagnosis, in 2009, he passed away.

Nancy didn't just sit and grieve. She wanted to help other kids, giving them a better chance so they wouldn't suffer the way Jacob did. And she was someone who could. Nancy is a lawyer, and she has a master's degree in government. She knows how to change things. And her family's tragedy gave her the energy to tackle the biggest problems with getting the best treatment for kids with cancer. The problems were these:

How can America encourage private drug companies to make new drugs for kids?
How can the thousands of drugs being invented for adults with cancer be made available for kids?

So Nancy started an organization called Kids v Cancer—kids against cancer. Its goal was to get drug companies to make more drugs and to make them available to doctors treating those kids. She trained herself in the specific kind of law that has to do with drugs: administrative law in the Food and Drug Administration (FDA). Instead of working on lawsuits and contracts—what we think of lawyers doing—Nancy studied the ins and outs of regulations, and she learned what it's like to write a bill for Congress to pass.

As a lawyer myself, that's what I do. While people like to make fun of lawyers, we all need them. We're a nation of laws, and that requires people who understand those laws. Nancy is one of them, and she's a great example of how much good a knowledge of law can do.

But here's a warning: It's complicated. Changing the world means more than just marching and having a great slogan. It means understanding politics and writing legislation. It takes incredible patience. In our case, it also took some really smart kids. I'll get to that in a bit.

Nancy decided to look at a law that already existed. Passed in 2007, it gave drug companies help in making new drugs for tropical diseases. The problem was, drugs are incredibly expensive to develop and get approved by the government. The companies have to pay for the scientists and laboratories, run many tests, then run more tests required by the Food and Drug Administration to make sure the drugs are safe and effective. A single drug can cost over $2 billion before it gets approved. And then what if the disease is fairly rare, or the people suffering from that disease aren't wealthy? The company can lose money. So Congress came up with a law that makes it easier to develop drugs for those tropical diseases. If a company created a new drug, the FDA would give it a voucher—an agreement to speed up approval of a *different* drug. The company that wins the voucher could then sell it to a different company. Each voucher can be worth as much as $300 million. This way, the drug company that sold the voucher could make money even if its tropical-disease drug loses money. The other company, the one that bought the voucher, could then sell *its* new drug faster and make more money. Everybody wins. Meanwhile, the taxpayers and patients don't have to pay higher prices or government money.

I told you it was complicated. Government is complicated.

What's more, the tropical disease voucher program didn't work as well as people wanted. When the bill got passed into law in 2007, not many companies used it. Nancy thought it was a good idea, but it needed fixing before it might work for childhood cancer. So she talked to every expert she could. She went to drug companies, biotech companies, Wall Street, investment experts, healthcare economists, members of Congress and their staffers.

People thought she was wasting her time. Her boy had just died, she wasn't an expert in that kind of law, she didn't know how to write a bill, and she had never lobbied

Congress before. But she had a mission. She got lawyers in a Washington law firm to work with her *pro bono*—for free. (Pro bono means "for the good" in Latin.) They helped her write a bill that created vouchers for drug companies to develop medicines for childhood cancer.

Then she got some lobbyists to help her for free. Staffers with two senators, a Democrat and a Republican, signed on to help. Nancy told them she had never had a meeting on the Hill before. "I'll be your political guide," one of the staffers told her.

Nancy learned that she faced a big uphill battle. Only one out of every 50 bills in Congress gets passed and signed into law by the President. One out of 50. That's not very good odds.

Plus, you can't just send a bill to Congress and say, "Here, pass this." You need members to sponsor it. Most of the time, you have to have sponsors in the House and Senate committees responsible for that part of government. In the House of Representatives, that committee is Energy and Commerce. I wasn't on that committee myself. I was Chairman of the Homeland Security Committee, which meant I had to lobby my colleagues on the Energy and Commerce Committee to cosponsor the bill with me. It was called the Creating Hope Act.

So Nancy had a bill written. I introduced it. We had sponsors in both the House and the Senate. But the odds weren't good. The Creating Hope Act was an experiment. I didn't know whether it would work or not. Democrats didn't like the bill because it would help drug companies,

164

and Republicans didn't like the bill because it didn't help drug companies enough. Certainly, everyone wanted to support research to fight childhood cancer; they just were having a hard time agreeing on how to do that.

Nancy called my wife, Linda. She chairs the childhood cancer committee at MD Anderson Cancer Center at the University of Texas, the number one cancer center in the nation. "I don't think this is going to pass," Nancy told Linda. "We don't have the votes."

Linda said, "We're going to pass this bill." She knew that the way to win was to change the question. "It's not about whether this helps or hurt drug companies," she said. "It's about the children. It's whether each member of Congress is for the children." If they said no, "they'll have to answer to me."

You have to understand my wife. I first met her at an event at the Air & Space Museum in Washington, when I went up to an attractive woman and introduced myself. I told her I was a prosecutor for the Justice Department and gave her my card. "So what do you do?"

"I'm an oceanographer, and I track Soviet submarines for Naval Intelligence."

I said, "Wow, I've never met a woman who tracks Soviet submarines. Would you like to go out with me?" I thought, *This is the coolest person I have ever met.* And a woman who doesn't lose.

For the Creating Hope Act, Linda did some of the lobbying personally, catching members as they went off the floor. To win this bill, to get it through Congress, we needed lobbyists. But here was another problem. Washington has plenty of them. It's hard for a new cause to make itself heard. Just to give you one example: Labor unions have lobby days when they flood Capitol Hill with 20,000 union members. Cancer advocacy groups were small and not well organized back then. We'd be lucky to get 200 people to lobby. So what could we do?

We thought about what Linda had said: *It's about the children.* We decided that, instead of thousands of adults, we'd send a few kids into their offices. Just kids. No adults. At first, the members wondered why these children were showing up. Adults think of kids as not that smart—that they just sit around watching *SpongeBob SquarePants* and playing games on their devices. But when the kids spoke, they proved how informed and persuasive they could be about a very complicated issue.

We got 30 kids to lobby for the Creating Hope Act. They went up to some of the most resistant members of Congress and their staff. Among them were friends of Nancy's son Jacob, along with Jacob's brother. Many of the kids have fought cancer themselves. We sent them into offices and made hardened Senators and House members cry. I even brought a few kids onto the floor of the House, which is technically against the rules. You're only allowed to bring your own kids. So I just said I had adopted these young lobbyists.

One of those kids, Brianna Commerford, was especially effective. At 13 years old, she was optimistic and articulate. Linda and I brought her onto the House floor and pointed to a member of Congress. "See that lady?" I told Brianna. "That's Nancy Pelosi, Speaker of the House. She's a big fish." The Speaker is one of the most powerful people in government. She is third in line after the Vice President if something happens to the President. And she decides what bills get voted on.

I said to Brianna, "Ask the Speaker if she will cosponsor our bill." This wasn't exactly following the rules, either. The Speaker usually doesn't cosponsor bills. So here we were bringing kids to the floor and asking the Speaker to violate tradition. Not to mention lobbying right where members of Congress vote. Another rule breaker.

Brianna marched right up to Nancy Pelosi and asked.

"Okay," Speaker Pelosi said. "I don't usually do that. But I'll do it for you."

That took care of the Democratic side. Then we had to work on the Republicans. Linda stood in front of the men's room and blocked the way until some of the reluctant members talked to her. And, despite the odds against it, the bill passed. The Senate followed suit, the President signed it, and drug companies began using vouchers to develop new drugs and to make drugs available for kids with cancer.

Since then, the FDA has approved 19 cancer drugs, including two specifically for childhood cancer.

Sure, the whole process takes time, and it can be frustrating. Advocates held more than 500 meetings to get that act passed. And some interest groups spend millions of dollars trying to get a bill passed, only to see it get stuck in a House or Senate committee. On the other hand, Nancy Goodman thinks that Kids v Cancer spent less than $20,000 on photocopying handouts and sometimes buying the kids lunch.

Think about it: 30 dedicated kids, a few activists, and some members of Congress pushed through a new law that jumpstarts research and treatments for kids with cancer. And they proved that democracy really works—even now.

During that time, I decided to hold a summit of leaders in the childhood cancer movement. We brought in top people in medicine, members of Congress, leading advocates, and some of the kids. This was ten years ago, and we've been holding it every year since then.

One of the great advocates, Mike Gillette—Sadie calls him Mr. Mike—runs a documentary film studio for the organization The Truth 365. He makes incredible videos of kids talking about their cancer experience. He's won Emmy awards for his films, which is a big deal. Plus, you can start a Truth 365 Club at your school to help make kids aware of childhood cancer. Mr. Mike is a talent scout for articulate kids. Whenever Nancy Goodman needed a kid to lobby a particular member of Congress, she would ask Mike. One day, Nancy said to him, "I need someone from Texas. Who do you have?"

Mike said, "I've got just the kid." He sent her videos he had done with Sadie. Nancy knew immediately that Sadie was a star. She just jumps off the screen in those videos.

Sadie and I first met when Annette Leslie introduced us at the Golden Toast, and then we really connected when Sadie and her mother visited me in my office. That's when I took the afternoon off to show her the Capitol. And we've been close friends ever since. Sadie has a spark to her, even when she's talking about her Hard Time. As Arthel Neville said when she interviewed Sadie and me on television, "I was immediately attracted to your light and your positivity." Everyone is.

When Sadie first came to Capitol Hill, she was in remission and on a mission. She has helped me get the Creating Hope Act reauthorized three times. The law has a "sunset" clause in it, meaning it expires after a certain period. It's set to expire again in the fall of 2020. We're now working to make the law permanent.

But the Creating Hope Act wasn't enough. We needed to make sure that companies developing adult cancer drugs didn't just research adults. They needed to study the drugs on kids with the same diseases. There already was a law that required drug companies to include kids in research. But that law had loopholes that excused the companies from cancer research. Nancy Goodman sprang into action again, spending a whole year on re-searching the issue. She and her allies wrote a new bill called the RACE for Children Act. The RACE part stands for Research to Accelerate Cures and Equity, which is exactly what it is supposed to make happen.

By now, people knew us. The Childhood Cancer Caucus was in place. We had our kid lobbyists. People didn't think we were just a flash in the pan. But the problem I had was, the drug companies really didn't want this bill, and they fought to water it down every way they could. Still, we had a lot of allies. The FDA supported our bill. The science magazines *Nature* and *Science* wrote positive stories about how important the law would be to jumpstart research on childhood cancer medicines. Plus, we had important Republican support in the Senate, such as Marco Rubio.

And we had the kids, including Sadie. She and her mother hit the Hill like the most positive storm. Kids v Cancer created Climb the Hill days, sending teams of children every two months. The kids get trained by other kids who have had experience with lobbying. Sadie has been a youth leader several times.

The bill passed with just the language we wanted, and the President signed it into law in 2017. The Creating Hope for Children Act gave drug companies an incentive to do the research. Now the RACE for Children Act required it.

And still we weren't done.

The money wasn't enough. Sadie and I went on television to talk about the need to increase funding for childhood cancer. As she likes to say, "We're worth more than four percent." And while we've increased the total pot of money, we still need to do more.

Now an organization of organizations, the Alliance for Childhood Cancer, wrote a bill called the STAR Act. Its full name was the Childhood Cancer Survivorship, Treatment, Access, and Research Act, and it was the most important childhood cancer bill ever written. It was a huge effort on the part of hundreds of cancer organizations, spearheaded by St. Baldrick's—the group that has people shave their heads. St. Baldrick's gives more money for research on childhood cancer than anybody except the federal government. The person who led the effort, Danielle Leach, has been working on the fight against cancer just about since she graduated from college. Her sister, Noel, was diagnosed with cancer 35 years ago; she's a survivor today. As if there wasn't enough cancer in Danielle's life, 25 years after her sister was diagnosed, Danielle's son Mason was diagnosed with medulloblastoma—brain cancer. To her surprise, Mason was given the same cancer drugs that Danielle's sister had been taking a quarter-century before. The dosages and combinations had changed, she says, "but the arsenal was the same. It was incredibly frustrating." Mason passed away at age five. Danielle was committed to getting laws like the STAR Act to change the treatments, making it so that other kids don't end up with the same drugs—and that they do have more hope for survival.

The STAR Act orders the National Institutes of Health to promote research on the childhood cancers that have the least effective cures—the diseases that basically are death sentences. The bill puts a pediatric oncologist on the board at the National Cancer Institute so that childhood cancer has a voice at the table when big decisions are made about how to fund research. And it helps promote the quality of life for the half-million kids who are cancer survivors; two-thirds of them face serious lifelong conditions. At the same time, the bill authorizes the Centers for Disease Control and Prevention to give money to state cancer registries, so scientists could do a better job of tracking childhood cancer kids and their survivorship rates. This is where research can really take off—and it reminds me of something.

Years ago, I was a federal prosecutor, working to bring justice to terrorists after the September 11th attacks. The reason those attacks happened was the fact that different law enforcement and intelligence agencies—state, federal, FBI, CIA and the like—weren't collaborating enough. They weren't sharing information. I hope that with the STAR Act, researchers can find it easier to share their discoveries and their data.

Plus, the bill increases funding for the National Institutes of Health by $150 million over five years, all to look for new cures. And those registries? They let the government use data to track all kinds of patterns and find ways to advance treatments.

A few months before the STAR Act passed the House of Representatives, Sadie introduced me at a rally of more than 1,000 people on Washington's National Mall. It was a beautiful September evening during Curefest. Sadie, standing next to Lily Weaver, gave me a pair of golden gloves to knock out cancer; I now display them proudly in the living room of my home.

Then Mike Gillette of The Truth 365 spoke. He surprised me by calling me "a man who has gone above and beyond anyone in history on that Capitol Hill" to help the cause of childhood cancer. He pointed toward Congress's beautiful, lit-up building while the crowd cheered. That's the sort of thing that can really go to person's head, and I admit I was feeling pretty proud. But at the same time, I knew these people weren't just cheering me. They were cheering for themselves. This cause, the cause of childhood cancer, had become a powerful movement.

Soon after, I gave a speech to encourage my fellow members of Congress to vote for the STAR Act. Behind me stood a picture of Sadie and me on the Speaker's Balcony. In the picture, we're looking past the clouds toward the sunlight coming through. That's what the STAR Act represented to me: sunlight for the children.

Then, in the summer of 2018, with Sadie standing beside him in the White House Oval Office, the President signed the bill into law. Instead of handing me the pen, he handed it to Sadie. I loved that.

The STAR Act had not only passed Congress easily, it was fully funded—entirely paid for. And this was the most comprehensive cancer bill ever passed. It's hard to pass a bill and have it signed into law. It's harder to get Congress to pay for legislation when they pass it. And it's even rarer to pass a bill that saves the lives of our greatest investment, our children.

There's a big moral to this story. CNN's Wolf Blitzer said it in an interview with Sadie and me right after the STAR Act passed: "Liberals and conservatives, because of people like you, they got together and they did something very special that's going to help a lot of kids." At a time when it looks like nothing can get done in Congress, when Washington is seen as broken, so partisan and toxic, we can still reach agreement on important things. Citizens can still get together and form a movement and get their elected officials to listen. And members of Congress can show they are human beings with families of their own. A child telling a cancer story can still get those members to think, *This is why I came to Washington.*

Now advanced, personalized medicine is being made available to children with cancer, while more drugs are getting developed. Money is becoming much more available for pediatric cancer research. And the vouchers are enabling drug companies to focus on treatments without losing money. These new treatments—including a medicine called Unituxin, one of only three drugs approved by the government over the last 20 years specifically to treat kids with cancer—are saving lives.

I got to meet one of those kids, Rex Ryan. Diagnosed with stage four neuroblastoma—cancer in nerve cells that can spread throughout the body and kill most patients—Rex had been through a dozen rounds of radiation, seven rounds of chemo, a stem cell transplant, and more. He spent more than 200 nights in the hospital, mostly at Dell Children's Medical Center in my hometown of Austin. Thanks to the Creating Hope Act, little Rex got treated with Unituxin. I got to visit the three-year-old when he completed the treatment.

And CAR-T, a truly revolutionary therapy, also is starting to cure some kids. That's the treatment where doctors take killer T cells (the body's "soldiers," as Sadie calls them) out of the body and retrains them to attack cancer. Unlike chemicals and radiation, CAR-T personalizes medicine by using the patient's own immune system to attack the cancer itself. The therapy is still being studied, and right now it's used for children only when their cancer relapses. But it shouldn't be long before CAR-T gets used as the first treatment for kids with cancer.

Personalized medicine instead of poison: This means using the child's own cells and retraining them to attack the specific kind of cells making the kid sick. It's absolutely fascinating. And it holds out the promise of a treatment that's more natural and less toxic, with fewer side effects and far fewer long-term problems for the patients.

One of the first kids to receive CAR-T treatment, thanks to research sped along by our legislation, was a seven-year-old named Emily Whitehead. Diagnosed with the same kind of leukemia Sadie had, she went through all the treatments possible at the time. Luckily, a kind of CAR-T therapy called tisagenlecleucel (don't ask me to pronounce it) got approved for young patients. It saved Emily's life. She's now a beautiful, healthy teenager.

And still we're not done. While eight out of ten kids with cancer here in America survive their first five years after treatment, in developing countries, at least eight out of ten die—including 300,000 kids, nine out of ten, in Africa each year. As far as we know. Most African children with cancer never even see a doctor to get diagnosed in the first place. So I've been working to get Congress to support existing efforts by various groups to bring childhood cancer care to developing nations. In September 2018, the World Health Organization launched a global initiative for childhood cancer with the aim of reaching at least 60 percent survival rate for kids by 2030, saving an additional one million lives. St. Jude Children's Research Hospital, founded in 1962 by the famous actor Danny Thomas to fight childhood cancer and other life-threatening diseases, provided $15 million of initial funding.

Another group, Global HOPE—Hematology Oncology Pediatric Excellence—is bringing help to childhood cancer patients in sub-Saharan Africa. Global HOPE is a team that combines Texas Children's Hospital in Houston, the Bristol-Myers Squibb Foundation, and the Baylor College of Medicine, with a budget of $150 million over multiple years. It's led by a good friend of mine, Dr. David Poplack, former director of Texas Children's Cancer and Hematology Centers and a professor of pediatric oncology at Baylor. Global HOPE does lifesaving work in African countries. In Botswana, the team is taking on 450 kids with cancer every year, dramatically improving survival. In Malawi, where two-thirds of citizens are under age 24, Global HOPE is treating many of the 5,000 new childhood cancer cases each year. In Uganda, they're helping 7,000 cases a year. The plan is to train some 4,800 professionals in African countries—including doctors, nurses, pharmacists, pediatric surgeons, social workers, and other healthcare professionals. "We're not just caring for these children," Dr. Poplack says. "We're teaching their healthcare professionals as well—teaching them to be advocates with their local government leaders for children with cancer and their families. They need to speak to their parliaments and say, 'Here's what we need for kids with cancer.'"

To help this effort, I introduced the Global HOPE Act in December 2019, and I'm hopeful for passage by Congress in 2020. The law would help save children's lives in developing countries through partnerships among the federal government, the private sector, scientific institutions, and nonprofit groups. We know this strategy can work; we did it already with HIV/AIDS, creating partnerships that saved more than 17 million lives worldwide. The President of Botswana, whom I met at Texas Children's, told me that our HIV/AIDS effort had saved a generation from extinction.

Now we have the opportunity to save the next generation from the scourge of cancer. A kid's chance of survival should not be determined by their birthplace.

This is a dream built upon a dream, all coming true. I've spent my career protecting people, especially children, against threats. I prosecuted terrorists, tracked terrorism as chair of the Committee on Homeland Security in Congress, and started an Internet Crimes Against Children office. But what kills children more, terrorism or cancer? Cancer does. I stop threats. And cancer is a threat.

Thanks to the bravery and energy of kids and advocates, we are seeing huge, rapid advances in reducing the threat of childhood cancer. And now we're taking that cause to the rest of the world, starting with Africa. As I write this, Linda and I will be heading to Botswana to celebrate International Childhood Cancer Day with the first lady of Botswana. And Sadie will be with me. She and I are going to meet the children being helped by Global HOPE Initiative. Children suffer from cancer in Africa worse than anywhere on earth. Our mission will be to spread the word to people back in America, and to turn suffering into meaning.

I'll tell you a secret. When I first went on national television with Sadie, I was more nervous than she was. Here was this little girl under the glaring lights and cameras. Would she speak up, or clam up? But she was brilliant. Right then I knew she was going to be a leading face of the movement, and I couldn't have been prouder of her. I just threw her out there, and she was a pro—a little girl who rose to the occasion for a cause she strongly believes in, turning the worst kind of situation into the best.

I think about a picture Sadie painted when she was still going through treatment. She's lying in the hospital, curled up in her bed. There are dark colors around her, showing her mood and her state of health. It's the saddest picture. She looks gaunt and pale, without hair. But look outward to what surrounds the scene in that picture: The colors turn bright.

That's the most beautiful thing about us humans, our ability to turn suffering into meaning. After all, you can't have lightness without the dark. It's the duality of nature and the universe. Viktor Frankl, a great psychiatrist who survived the Holocaust death camps during World War II, wrote that "to live is to suffer." He also said, "If there is meaning in life at all, then there must be a meaning in suffering...Without suffering and death, human life cannot be complete." I think that the most human, and even heroic, thing you can do in life is to find that meaning in suffering, even in the death of those we love. Sometimes it takes a child like Sadie to teach us that.

Together, Sadie and all the other angels, the families and advocates and scientists, will fight with me to bring new cures to children around the world. We'll turn suffering into meaning. We'll encounter a great darkness along the way. But we know that the further we go, the more we'll picture a great future for these kids. It will have the most brilliant colors.

Michael McCaul

The Pictures

Here are just a few of the hundreds of pictures taken during and after my treatment. They're all by my family (mostly Mom) unless I say they're by Mr. Mike Gillette of TheTruth365.com.   −Sadie

Mom and me. I could have made the first picture here one of me getting the medicine. But this *is* me getting medicine: Mom's kiss. Our friend Miss Cassie took this picture after the first time she shaved my head. The chemo had made my hair fall out, then it grew back and wasn't supposed to fall out again. But then it did. I ended up getting shaved another six times!

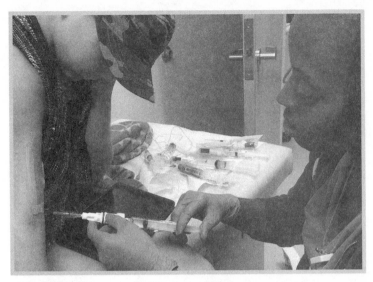

One of my favorite nurses, Christina, pushes methotrexate into my PICC line. I wore that camo hat every single day after my hair first fell out.

Me with Dad and brother Grant, the first time we marched up Capitol Hill at CureFest. Gold is the color of childhood cancer. And 4% is how much of the government's cancer research money goes to childhood cancer.

Congressman McCaul shows me the Speaker's Balcony before he takes me on a tour of the building. I'm wearing my favorite pink dress. The Congressman told me then that I could do anything. After all we've been through, all we got done, I believe him.

Sadie's Sleigh, 2018. Mom got up on the ladder to shoot this. These days, the toys cover the whole cul-de-sac our house is on. Last Christmas we gave away 20,500 toys.

Me with Lily and Vara. We called ourselves the Three Little Pigs, the Three Amigos, the Three Musketeers. Every time Lily or Vara relapsed, my heart broke a little more.

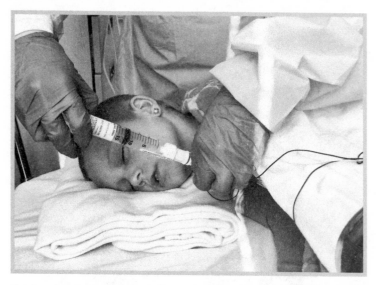

Getting chemo into my port before waking up from one of my 19 spinal tap procedures. The nurses would give me an infusion while I was still asleep to make it easier for me.

Lily and I watch while Congressman McCaul gets awarded a pair of Golden Gloves at CureFest, for leading the childhood cancer fight in Congress. All the cancer kids signed the gloves.

Lily with me at the Capitol, the day we lobbied Congress together. She was six years older, but when we were together, it was as if we were the same age. Even though we talked about some very hard things about childhood cancer with many members of Congress that day, Lily and I always had fun together.

The Congressman and I speak to reporters outside the White House right after the President signed the STAR Act, the bill I lobbied for. It's the biggest childhood cancer law of all, and I got to stand right next to the President when he signed it.

SADIE'S FIGHT

11-YEAR-OLD GIRL SCORES BIG VICTORY FOR CANCER PATIENTS

CAN'T COMMENT FURTHER   CNN.com   IN UNPRECEDENTED MOVE, U.N. ORD   WOLF

Congressman McCaul and I speak on CNN after the STAR Act became law. Wolf Blitzer, the interviewer, said, "Liberals and conservatives, because of people like you, they got together and they did something very special that's going to help a lot of kids." When I went to the airport right after that, someone recognized me. She had seen the interview on all the TVs there.

The famous photo of Lily and me, taken by Mr. Mike. She had comforted me all through my treatment, and then relapsed. Now it was my turn to support her.

Speaking at CureFest after my hair grew back for the last time. I'm usually shy at first, but can turn on this switch in my head. The switch makes me be a voice for all the kids who have had cancer, and for those still fighting.

The family at our Yellow Ball. Why yellow? Because it means happiness, positivity, optimism, youth, smiles—everything the Sadie Keller Foundation represents.

Grant, the world's best brother, has been with me at every CureFest I've gone to. He wants to become an oncologist to help cure kids with cancer. The Kids v Cancer on our sign is an organization that helped write some of the most important childhood cancer bills. Its founder, Nancy Goodman, introduced me to Congressman McCaul.

Congressman McCaul and me at the Candlelight Vigil. At CureFest in front of the White House, thousands of people carry candles to honor all of the children who have passed away from cancer. Tattoo Tom says each name, and everyone in the crowd repeats it. No child is forgotten.

The Angels

I wish I could include all the angels I've met as well as those I haven't, who had the energy and the courage to join the fight against childhood cancer. Here are some of them.   –Sadie

Alex Howard, my babysitter, who dropped everything when I was feeling the most down in the hospital.

Angela, **Krister**, **Ellie**, **Chloe**, **Lily**, and **Keagan Killinger**: A family we stay with when we travel to Washington, D.C. They have become our D.C. family.

Annette Leslie from the Carson Leslie Foundation, who organizes the Golden Toast. Her son Carson passed away from medulloblastoma when he was a teenager. He was the quarterback of his football team and shortstop for his baseball team. Before he passed away, he wrote a book. He died with one big bold wish: to help the next kid with cancer. Miss Annette is helping arrange research funding in Texas, and she does a lot to bring awareness nationally. She's the one who introduced me to Congressman McCaul.

Ariella Stein, a friend—and one of Lily Weaver's close friends—who passed away from cancer. Ariella and Lily are together in Heaven. Ariella started Ari's Bears (arisbears.org), taking bears to kids in hospitals. It continues to grow.

Around the Clock Movers and **Black Tie Moving Company** volunteer every year to move all the Sadie's Sleigh toys to hospitals. They're like Santa's elves, only much bigger.

Aunt Erica and **Uncle Ben**, and **Aunt Amy** and **Uncle Drew**. They were there for my parents, and they helped with Grant so that he didn't have to stay at the hospital all the time. Aunt Erica, and my cousins Ella and Sophie, came to the hospital when I was there forever. They were there when I got to dye my hair bright pink. They cheered me up when I needed it the most.

Ava Blaser, another one of my friends and fellow cancer fighters.

Avery Alford, one of my best non-cancer friends. We played on the same soccer team before I was diagnosed.

Avery Braden, the very first kid to receive a Milestone Gift.

Benjamin Landry, who got diagnosed with medulloblastoma at age five, after he collapsed while playing baseball. His treatments left him blind and deaf. But he just reached ten years in remission!

Bill Hutchinson, Dallas businessman and philanthropist. He supported the Sadie Keller Foundation Yellow Ball.

Brianna Commerford. She lobbied Congress before I did and went right up to the Speaker of the House to get her to co-sponsor the Creating Hope Act.

Brittany Lanier, one of my favorite nurses. She took me under her wing and made me laugh all the time. Every patient loves Brittany!

Brixton Henfield, a little girl with rhabdomyosarcoma who got a Milestone gift from us. We learned that Brixton had relapsed when we saw her at CureFest.

Caitlin Arndt, my Child Life specialist at Children's Medical Center in Dallas. Picture an angel who brings you toys and makes you feel better just with her words and her smile. And I love her pet therapy dog, Blair.

Cameron Lee, my friend who went with me to the hospital after I was first diagnosed and sat next to me when I got blood drawn. Having a friend with me made me braver.

Cassie Haynes, our hairstylist friend who dyed my hair pink before I lost it all. And she was the first person to shave my head.

Childhood Cancer Caucus, including current and former Members of Congress Michael Burgess, G.K. Butterfield, Rosa DeLauro (love her purple hair!) Chris Van Hollen, Mike Kelly, Jackie Speier, and Deborah Pryce. And, of course, Michael McCaul.

Christian and **Danielle Hage**, friends from Covenant Church who have helped us with the Yellow Ball and were there for my family during the Hard Time.

Christian Weeresinghe. I hadn't met this amazing kid before, but he heard me give a talk at Covenant Church and then went off and raised $25,000 for the Sadie Keller Foundation!

Coco, my little dog. Like many dogs, she can tell when a kid has cancer and gave me major love medicine.

Congressman McCaul's family: **Linda**, **Avery**, **Caroline**, **Michael**, **Jewel**, and **Lauren**.

Cousins Sophie Atkinson, **Ella Atkinson**, **Charlie Atkinson**, **Abby Fisher**, **Sam Fisher**; and **Devin**, **Megan**, **Riley**, **Lilly**, and **Stella Keller**.

Covenant Church in Carrollton, Texas. We went to another church before I got cancer. Covenant Church asked me to speak and welcomed us, and my family found our home. I enjoy all the activities and love going every week.

Danielle Leach, Director of Government Relations and Advocacy, St. Baldrick's, one of the big childhood cancer groups. Miss Danielle recruited kids to lobby, and she led the way for the STAR Act, one of the biggest bills to bring research for childhood cancer treatments.

David Arons of the National Brain Tumor Society. It's an organization that gives money for research. And Mr. Arons is one of a team of advocates working to increase funding for childhood cancer from the Defense Department.

Dean Crowe of the Rally Foundation for Childhood Cancer. It raises millions of dollars for research. She's also working to increase funding for childhood cancer from the Defense Department.

Dena Sherwood of the cancer-fighting foundation Arms Wide Open. A good friend of ours, she puts on CureFest and operates The Truth 365 with Mr. Mike. Her son, Billy, was diagnosed with neuroblastoma and went through years of very hard treatment. He is in remission and doing well. Now Miss Dena funds millions of dollars for cancer research, including finding new treatments for neuroblastoma.

Dick Vitale, the famous ESPN sportscaster who asked me to be part of his All Courageous Team at his gala each year. He has raised more than $35 million for childhood cancer research with the V Foundation. And he's my friend.

Dr. Engel (not her real name), the best oncologist ever. No matter what I had going on, she always lifted my spirits and made me feel better.

Erika Elrod, a volunteer and board member for the Sadie Keller Foundation. Miss Erika has helped us from the beginning. Her daughters, Ava and Bella, have become my friends, and they advocate for childhood cancer.

Fatima Gonzalez, my phlebotomist who draws my blood. She's the kindest, nicest friend, which says a lot considering that she poked me a million times.

Flick Blevins, a fellow cancer kid. When I saw him handing out cupcakes to the nurses, that gave me the idea to get baking.

Gavin Lindberg of the Edward P. Evans Foundation. Mr. Lindberg works to increase funding for research on childhood leukemia.

Grandma Sherry and **Grandpa Jim**, who left Iowa and moved to Texas to help our family when I was diagnosed.

Grant, the best brother in the world, who was always there for me and still is today. He always makes me laugh. Grant wants to be a pediatric oncologist.

Hunter Oney, a boy with lymphoma. We gave him headphones as a Milestone Gift and later learned he was back in the hospital for terrible pain. Today he's in remission and in college.

Jamie Decker, my dad's friend, an inspirational speaker who told the story about the Butterfly Effect.

Jennifer Arthur from the Children's Cancer Fund, a Dallas cancer foundation that gives millions for research and supports Child Life at my hospital. They do a fashion show during their gala each year. I was a feature model in 2016 and had the best time.

Jennifer Flynn of Kids v Cancer, the organization that pulls together child lobbyists like me and was with me the day I met with Congressman McCaul. Jenn sets up all my meetings when I lobby.

Jennifer Maness, our social worker from the hospital. She's been with us from the beginning.

Jim Allison, the scientist who made big discoveries in immunotherapy, which offers hope for cures that don't poison cancer fighters. He won the Nobel Prize for it.

Julia Brown, the first cancer kid friend I met after being diagnosed.

Kathleen Ruddy, CEO of the St. Baldrick's Foundation.

Katy Blakey, a Dallas TV reporter who became more than a reporter to me. She became a good friend.

Kcee Blevins, Flick's mom, who taught me a lot about baking.

Kelly Brown, one of my favorite nurses. She knew what it was like to be a cancer kid; she had been one herself. She then had a beautiful baby boy who got cancer and passed away.

Kelly Zindel, the woman at the front desk at school. Her son, Kincaid, finished his treatment for a brain tumor the same day I was diagnosed. Her daughter, Maddie, is my friend. Kelly helped our family a lot when I was first diagnosed.

Kevin Mathis, who works with St. Baldrick's and helped to get the STAR Act passed by Congress.

Kiki Keating and **Jay Heinrichs**, along with his partners at Gavia Books. They showed me what it takes to make a book and put it in bookstores, which is a lot of work. And Kiki is making sure everyone knows about *BETTER ANGELS*.

Kristin Jenkins and **Miss Katie Forsythe** volunteer with the Sadie Keller Foundation, and they lead our Milestone gift program. I am so grateful for them!

LeAnna Headley, who started Our Amazing Fighters to raise awareness of childhood cancer.

Lilly Armbruster, little Lilly, who came to my End of Chemo party and later passed away from cancer.

Lily Weaver, one of my best friends that I have ever made in my whole life. We did a lot of photos and videos with The Truth 365 to raise awareness for childhood cancer and had so much fun together. She relapsed twice with Ewing's sarcoma and passed away soon before we finished this book.

Linda McCaul, Congressman McCaul's wife. She chairs the childhood cancer committee at MD Anderson Cancer Center at the University of Texas. This is the place doing some of the most exciting cancer research.

Louie the Christmas dog. He cuddles with me whenever I'm feeling down. Or happy.

Luke Grumbles, a cancer friend I met in the hospital. We raced cars after the Sadie's Sleigh Toy Shop. He passed away from acute myeloid leukemia (AML).

Make-A-Wish Foundation. They sent my entire family to Australia for two weeks. Whenever I was feeling terrible in the hospital, my doctor and nurses would tell me to think about what I wanted to wish for.

Maria Bisceglia, my amazing nurse practitioner. I call her a mini Dr. Engel.

Mark and **Cindy Pentecost**, owners of It Works Global. My mom is part of this company, and they have been praying for me and my family since my diagnosis. They have also supported Sadie's Sleigh since my first year. Mr. Mark was going through cancer the same time as me, and we would always send each other videos and prayers.

Matt Fleeger and **Tim Taylor** from Gulf Coast Western, who donate all the toys for our Sadie's Sleigh Toy Shop at the hospital. These are the best of the best toys. They also give us hundreds of toys for Sadie's Sleigh every year.

Mehrdad Moayedi, a Dallas businessman and friend, who has always been there and supported me and my family through the hard time. He now supports the Sadie Keller Foundation. His business, Centurion American, has sponsored every one of our fundraising events.

Michael McCaul, my close friend and a member of Congress who pushed through laws that are getting support for childhood cancer research. He's also the person who made this book possible.

Mike Gillette of The Truth 365, which creates videos and photos of cancer kids and raises awareness for the cause. I love to work with Mr. Mike. He has helped give me a platform to have my voice heard for childhood cancer.

Mimi and **Pop**, who dropped everything in San Antonio to come see me in the hospital as soon as I was diagnosed. Pop was the first person to notice how pale I was when we visited them the weekend before I was diagnosed. They would come to Dallas often to see me since we couldn't go there.

Moore Supply, a plumbing supply business where my dad works. They took care of him after I was diagnosed so he could be with me when I was getting my chemo.

My parents, **Sarah** and **Shawn**, who have been just as strong as me. They are the reason I got through all this. I'm grateful for everything they have done for me and Grant.

My pastors, **Stephen** and **Erika Hayes** at Covenant Church. Pastor Stephen asked me to speak at services, and they're now friends who have done a lot for our family and the foundation.

Nancy Goodman, who founded Kids v Cancer after her son Jacob died of cancer. She wrote one of the most important cancer bills, the Creating Hope Act, and helps pull together child lobbyists for the cause.

Nurse **Christina**, my nurse almost every week for chemo at the clinic. We became close friends, and she came to the hospital for my last chemo even though she was off duty.

Nurses **Brittany**, **Coco**, **Jen**, **Kelly**, and **Lane**. They acted like angels all the time, making me feel better even when they were poking me. They were the most loving people you could possibly meet.

Pamela Moayedi is a friend who has supported me and my family through the end of my treatment, and she's helped with the Sadie Keller Foundation.

Pink Heals firefighters, police and medics. They visit cancer kids and make them feel like the center of the universe, and they did it for me.

Rebecca Butler, M.D., my pediatrician who found something wrong with my blood and sent me for tests.

Ryan Seacrest, the celebrity who sets up professional broadcasting studios in hospitals for kids to use.

Sadie Murata, Sadiebug, my good friend, cancer fighter and fellow advocate, who passed away. Sadie always said: "Life is a gift, so use it wisely." These are words we all should live by.

Senators **Lamar Alexander**, **Michael Bennett**, **Bob Casey**, **Johnny Isaacson**, and **Marco Rubio**. They've led the fight for childhood cancer in the U.S. Senate.

Sierra Faulkner. Three-year-old Sierra had Ewing's sarcoma that made her blind, but radiation therapy made her able to see. We gave her a giant castle for a Milestone Gift.

Stephanie and **Steve Seay**, great friends of our family. They brought us meals when I was first diagnosed and now support my foundation.

Stephanie, **Steve**, **Mahri**, and **Kenzie Baker**, our neighbors and friends who have done so much for us and have become like family. They made a huge "Welcome Home" sign and put it on our garage for when I got home from the hospital.

Summer Cernock, another cancer fighting friend.

Tamara Quilty, who helps the Sadie Keller Foundation and was a big part of Sadie's Sleigh. Without her, we wouldn't have been able to collect 20,500 toys this past winter!

Tattoo Tom Mitchell, who started the cancer-fighting organization StillBrave after his beautiful teenage daughter, Shayla, died of cancer. Tattoo Tom leads the march every year at CureFest.

Tatum Foster, my friend who tried on wigs with me and joined me at CureFest. Tatum ended up getting secondary cancer, caused by the chemo from her first cancer. She is currently in remission.

Tatum Lander, of my best non-cancer friends. It was at her birthday sleepover where everyone asked me questions about what cancer was like. Tatum and I always have fun together.

Thomas Rice works with Congressman McCaul on the most important bills, including childhood cancer.

Tim and **Donna Culliver**, great advocates who got Congressman McCaul involved in the movement. The Cullivers run Adam's Angels Ministry, which helps families of children with cancer with expenses, meals, transportation, and hospital parking fees. And just as important, Angel volunteers come and give company and prayers. Their little boy Adam passed away from AML leukemia at age four, just four days after he was diagnosed.

Tina Amin, Sadie Keller Foundation volunteer and board member. She has been a huge help and support over the years.

Todd Tenholder, Michael McCaul's childhood friend who died of cancer.

Tony Colton, a friend who passed away from cancer. I met him at the Dick Vitale gala. Tony was positive and always nice to me. He advocated a lot for kids with cancer so that others didn't have to go through what we did.

Uncle Heath and **Aunt Lori** and **Uncle Josh** and **Aunt Jamie**, who were there for Dad and our family during my treatment.

Vara James. She had Wilms tumor, a kind of kidney cancer. She's the girl who did the Bohemian Rhapsody video with me, before relapsing. She's one of my best friends.

White Pants Agency. They created our website, sadiekellerfoundation.org, and they help us in all kinds of ways.

... And all those who have been there for me and my family, prayed for kids with cancer, or supported research for childhood cancer:

Thank you!

The Words

This list isn't something to read all through unless you really want to. You can use it to help with technical medical things or political words. And you can find the organizations and events you might want to join. But I also used some of the words in this list to put down some thoughts that didn't fit in my story.   –Sadie

6MP Mercaptopurine, a cancer-fighting drug. It makes you lose weight, turn pale, and feel tired all the time.

Action Mode What my family goes into during an emergency. Some people curl up or hide when things go wrong. Some people pretend nothing happened. Other people get jumping. That's my family, especially my mother. People talk about how police and soldiers run toward the sound of gunfire. Mom runs toward me whenever there's trouble. Come to think of it, so do nurses. They're all heroes.

Acute If we're talking cancer, it means "this just happened and it's happening fast." The cancer is growing quickly, creating lots of baby blood cells called blasts.

Advocate An angel who works for childhood cancer cures.

ALL Acute lymphoblastic leukemia, which is what I had. It's a kind of blood cancer that happens mostly to kids. Grownups hardly ever get it. The kind I had, B-cell, turned the white blood cells in my bone marrow into cancer zombies that kept on living and living and making more of the same cells. It's the most common kind of ALL. Most but not all kids who get treated for this survive it.

AML Acute myelogenous leukemia, a type of blood cancer that's less common in kids than ALL. While the treatment is different, most kids with AML will live. At least in America. Both AML and ALL start in the bone marrow, just with different cells.

ANC Absolute neutrophil count. This is the number of good white blood cells, the kind that fight off bacteria and keep you healthy. A normal kid has between 5,000 and 10,000 of these cells.

Anesthesia Medicine that makes you not feel much or anything at all. Some kinds of anesthesia don't put you to sleep; it just relaxes your muscles, takes away the pain, or makes you forget you ever felt pain. Other kinds of anesthesia put you under, meaning you fall asleep and wake up after the doctors are done doing whatever they needed to do.

Anesthesiologist A doctor who specializes in giving you medicine that makes you not feel pain or keeps you asleep during surgery.

Angel Angels come in all kinds, and lots of people in many religions have believed in them. The angel in the Bible named Michael is an archangel—meaning a Very Important Angel. A VIA is the very best kind of VIP. To me, humans who act like angels are angels, because they do the sorts of things that angels in Heaven would do. These things can even lead to miracles. Michael McCaul, who was named after the Archangel Michael, is one of the angels in my life. He started the Childhood Cancer Caucus, which is leading to medical miracles. He's definitely a VIA. But not all the angels I've known are VIAs. Some are just beautiful, innocent children, some of the nicest people I've ever met, who got cancer and went to Heaven. They inspire those of us who survived to do the best we can to be angels ourselves.

Antibiotics   Medicines that kill germs.

Antibody   A big protein molecule that kills bacteria and viruses.

Antigen   A molecule that a T cell and antibodies sniff out. A vaccine is basically just a bunch of antigens that don't do anything harmful. When you get vaccinated, the antigens make your immune system—antibodies, T cells—take action.

Asthma   It's when a person has trouble breathing or coughs a lot. It can be caused by all kinds of things, such as an allergy. Mom says I had asthma when I was a baby, and we figured that was causing my problems on the soccer field. Which turned out to be cancer, not asthma.

B-cell   A kind of white blood cell. In the kind of cancer that I had, the B-cells got out of control.

Bag of blood   These days it's not exactly blood, but the stuff you need most that's taken from blood—like red or white blood cells, platelets, or plasma, which is the liquid part of the blood. The bag gets hung from your IV pole and the blood stuff flows through a tube and into your body. People donated the blood that was used for me. If people didn't donate blood, kids like me would be in big trouble.

Benadryl   A kind of antihistamine, meaning it stops allergies. It comes in different kinds. You can swallow it, or it can come in cream form to spread on your skin.

When I got an allergic reaction to platelets—the stuff in my bag of blood—the nurse gave me Benadryl.

Bill   Something that wants to become a law. A bill gets "drafted," or written, by a lobbyist or expert or congressional staffer. It gets talked about and rewritten in a committee. The committee votes whether to accept it. Then it goes to the other house of Congress. Both houses—the House of Representatives and the Senate—vote on their own bill. Then each house's bill goes into "markup," where they decide the language of the combined bill. Then both houses vote all over again, and if a majority in each house says yes, then the bill goes to the President. He has to agree to sign it before it can become law. Only one out of every 50 bills ever becomes a law. So you can see how amazing it was that the STAR Act, which I lobbied for, became an actual law. Legislation is really, really hard, but it's worth the effort. The law I worked on is saving lives.

Biopsy   This is when doctors take a piece of your body, and it's looked at in the lab. They can use a needle, or a tiny vacuum, or an endoscope—a teeny camera with a grabber called forceps. When doctors biopsied my bone marrow, it didn't hurt. I was asleep.

Blasts   Baby blood cells. "Blasts" is short for myeloblasts. In a kid with leukemia, the cells act like Peter Pan, never growing up. They just keep splitting and making more blasts.

Blessing   A gift that graces your life. Blessings often don't seem like blessings until you see them in the right way. For me, cancer turned out to be a blessing in a scary Halloween disguise.

Blood count The measurement of the health of your blood. It counts things like red and white blood cells called neutrophils, hemoglobin (it's what carries oxygen in red blood cells), and platelets.

Blood disorders Anything that goes wrong with your blood, duh. Leukemia is a blood disorder.

Blood pressure The pressure of blood against the walls of your arteries. Think about a garden hose. Turn the spigot all the way up, and the pressure in the hose gets high. Turn it lower, lower pressure. When someone measures your blood pressure, you get two numbers. One is for when your heart beats, the other is for when your heart is resting between beats. (The numbers are for systolic and diastolic, but you don't have to know that unless you plan to go into medicine like my brother, Grant.) A kid in elementary school should have a reading of around 115 over 80.

Bloodwork The work of drawing and testing your blood. The results are also called bloodwork: "Let me take a look at your bloodwork."

Bone marrow The gooey stuff inside most of your bones. It makes red blood cells and white blood cells. Some kids with leukemia get bone marrow transplants—really, stem cell transplants, which make good blood cells.

Brain tumor A mess of cells that don't do what they're supposed to. Brain tumors come in two main kinds:

malignant (bad), meaning cancer; and benign (not bad), meaning not cancer. Even benign tumors can do bad things, like cause terrible headaches or build up and cause brain damage. Malignant tumors often spread into the rest of the brain or the spinal cord. Brain cancer is the second most common kind of cancer that kids get, after leukemia. I've had friends who died from brain cancer. But many kids survive it. The odds depend on what kind of cancer a kid has.

Bravery You hear people say that being brave means not being scared. I think the bravest people are the ones who are scared the most and still do what they have to do. My mom is one of the bravest people I know, and she was the bravest she ever was when she was the most scared for me. When I give out Milestone Gifts to cancer fighters, I tell them how brave they are. Because they are. And telling them helps make them even braver.

Butterfly Effect Sensitive dependence on initial conditions. That means a tiny thing at the beginning can cause humongous changes in the long run. Like a butterfly flapping its wings in South America causing a tornado in Texas. A kind word can make just as big a difference.

Camp Esperanza A summer camp I went to for kids with cancer. There are a bunch of camps for "complex care" kids. You can Google "complex care medical summer camps" to learn more.

Cancer fighter Someone with cancer who fights it. I like to say that instead of "patient," because a patient just sounds like someone who lies around and waits, like, moaning and crying. A cancer fighter fights.

Cancer A disease caused by cells growing out of control, failing to die.

Capitol The building where Congress votes. It's very beautiful, and you can visit it. Ask your member of Congress if you can get a tour. Go to congress.gov/members to find your representative's contact information. People think you have to be rich or a lobbyist for some giant corporation or union, but the staff people in congressional offices are very friendly.

CAR-T A new kind of cancer treatment that uses T cells, the cells in your body that hunt down viruses and germs and things like that. Scientists change those cells in the laboratory so that they hunt down cancer. The CAR stands for Chimeric Antigen Receptor. "Chimeric" means something that's made of two different things, like genes. Receptors spot the antigens on foreign things in your body. In this case, the CAR sniffs cancer cells.

Caucus An interest group in Congress. The Childhood Cancer Caucus is one. It's made of members of Congress especially interested in childhood cancer.

Chemo Short for chemotherapy.

Chemotherapy A treatment with medicines to beat cancer, or whatever else you're sick from. Chemotherapy can last for months or more. Mine lasted two and a half years.

Child life specialist The coolest, nicest kind of person you will ever meet. The specialist helps you cope with scary things or pain and will bring you toys and cheer you up. She can also help your brother and can talk to your parents about how to deal with you if you're the patient. Child life specialists are college graduates, and many have a master's degree.

Childhood Cancer Awareness Month September. It lets people know about kids with cancer. That way everybody can know that cancer kills more kids than any other disease. Forty-three kids a day get diagnosed with cancer. Only four percent of money spent on research by the National Cancer Institute gets spent on childhood cancer. And the kid isn't the only person who suffers. Their families do, too. And the expenses can be horrifying. Just one hospital stay for a cancer kid can cost more than $40,000. Insurance doesn't always pay for all of it.

Childhood Cancer Summit Congressman McCaul and the other leaders of Congress's Childhood Cancer Caucus hold this summit every year in Washington, usually just before CureFest. It's where people come and talk about ways to fight childhood cancer. I've gotten to speak there. It's really important.

Children's Medical Center in Dallas The hospital where I got diagnosed and treated. It's the eighth biggest pediatric hospital in the country. Children's doesn't just treat cancer kids. That's just the sixth floor. It also does trauma care—like when a kid gets into a bad accident—as well as sports medicine, eating disorders, all kinds of things. I didn't like staying there (who likes being stuck in a hospital?), but they saved my life. And the nurses and doctors and child life specialists and everybody else are my heroes.

Chill pills   Just jelly beans. I put them in little medicine bottle sized jars and wrote a fake prescription. The amazing thing is, they really help. Take two chill pills when stressed. If you think they'll work in de-stressing you, then they'll work. Scientists call this the placebo effect. If you believe it will work, it often works. Belief makes miracles.

Chimeric   A monster mash. It just means two or more things combined into one. But the first chimera really were monsters. Look up Chimera on the web to see cool, disgusting, and scary pictures.

Choices   What you decide between. In America, we love choices. We walk down the potato chip aisle in a supermarket and see a zillion kinds. But kids get fewer choices, and so we don't always get the practice. We need to get good at easy choices—what kinds of clothes we wear, what food to eat, what kinds of books to read, whether we have to take computer lab—so that we can make the hard choices. Here's a hard choice: How to deal with cancer when you're seven. People will take care of you when you're sick. And they can try to cheer you up. But when it comes to your attitude, you're all alone. That's your choice. I chose to make the best of my cancer—which doesn't mean I was always all "Hey! It's a beautiful day!" When I was in the hospital, I curled up and cried and didn't want to go to the playroom. But in the long run, I tried to use my Hard Time to help other kids with theirs. That was my choice. The best, hardest choices turn into goals, which turn into the best lives.

Clinic This is where outpatients go. It's in the hospital, but you get to go home when you're done. I went there each week to get my treatments after I got out of the hospital.

Counts A sheet of paper filled with all your lab results. I would get one of these at every appointment with my lab results for that day.

CPR Cardiopulmonary resuscitation, which means keeping alive a person whose heart has stopped. Someone who is trained in CPR pushes on the victim's chest and also does mouth-to-mouth. If you're not trained, you're supposed to do the pushing without the mouth-to-mouth. First, somebody has to call 9-1-1. Then you push hard and fast right in the middle of the chest. A nurse told me that the perfect rhythm is songs like "Stayin' Alive" and "Dancing Queen." You can watch a video and see what other songs will work by going to nyp.org/cpr.

Creating Hope Act An important law that encourages drug companies to create new drugs for childhood cancer. You can learn about it at kidsvcancer.org. That's the group that first wrote the bill.

CT Computed tomography. Some people call it a CAT scan, for computed axial tomography. They're both the same thing, a machine that lets doctors see through your body. You lie in a big donut called a scanning ring. It takes X-rays all around you in a circle, showing a slice of your whole body. Then the X-ray beam moves and circles again for another slide right next to a first one. After taking lots of these pictures, a computer puts them all together. Then a doctor gets on a computer and can see all around and through the part he's looking at, including your organs, bones, and veins. You're in the machine for about 15 minutes to half an hour. It doesn't hurt or anything.

CureFest Every September, thousands of cancer fighters, families, and supporters come to Washington, D.C., to let Congress and the public know how important it is to fight childhood cancer. It's amazing and fun, and the climax is a march up to Capitol Hill. You don't have to be a cancer fighter yourself to come. Go to the website CureFestusa.org to find out more about attending. (You'll see me and Congressman McCaul in the video!) CureFest is fun and inspiring and can save lives. You should come!

Cyclophosmamide A cancer drug that makes you lose your hair. Plus, wounds like the one for my port don't heal as well. It also causes nausea and low blood counts. You can't leave the house when you're on this chemo, because of the risk of infections.

Dexamethasone　A steroid that fights inflammation. Kids with ALL leukemia, including me, get it. It's really important in fighting cancer. One of the things it does is to keep you from throwing up, which can happen from chemotherapy. So I'm really really glad I got it. But it can cause roid rage. It made me not sleep, and instead of raging, I just cried a lot. And it makes you really, really hungry.

DI　Delayed Intensification. In a high-risk ALL leukemia patient like me, you go through different phases. First is induction, which is usually a month of chemo and the hardest phase. Next comes consolidation, which lasts another month or two. It means more chemo to wipe out the rest of the cells. Then comes interim maintenance: more chemo, about two months. Delayed intensification follows that, and it's when you get the same kind of high doses you got in the first phase. All of your hair falls out, including your lashes and eyebrows, and you don't get to go anywhere because the chemo wipes out your immune system. Finally there is maintenance, and you stay in this phase of chemo for the remaining year and a half.

Diagnosis　When doctors figure out what's wrong with you. It comes from Greek and Latin words meaning "apart" and "know." Which basically means a diagnosis says, "What's wrong with you is this and not that."

DIPG　Diffuse Intrinsic Pontine Glioma. An inoperable brain tumor in the brainstem. There is a 0% cure rate for this type of cancer. This is another reason Congressman McCaul and I fight for more research funding.

Doxorubicin   The Red Devil. This red liquid helps kill the cancer, but it makes most kids sick to their stomach. Not me, though. I was lucky. It also causes low blood counts and mouth sores, and it makes all of your hair fall out. I got Doxorubicin during DI.

Emla   A cream with lidocaine, which numbs pain. Mom spread it around my port to keep the wound from hurting.

ER   Emergency room. It's often called an emergency department, or ED. If you're a cancer kid, it's like you get a VIP pass. They zoom you right in so you don't get exposed to other people. But you have to wear a mask.

Ewing's sarcoma   A kind of cancer that's usually in and around the bones. Several of my friends have had Ewing's.

Food and Drug Administration (FDA)   The government agency that has to approve new drugs, to make sure they do more good than harm. Because of all the tests and approvals, it can take years for a drug to get approved. The Creating Hope Act gives vouchers, sort of like a special ticket, to drug companies who work on childhood cancer medicines. The companies can then sell the vouchers or use them to speed up approval for different drugs.

Foundation   A legal thing you set up so people can give money for a cause. The long name is charitable foundation. The Sadie Keller Foundation is a charitable foundation.

Global HOPE The HOPE stands for Hematology Oncology Pediatric Excellence. Hematology is about blood, oncology is about cancer, and pediatric is kids. Global HOPE brings medicine to cancer kids in Africa. Congressman McCaul is working to get Congress to support it with money.

Golden Toast This kicks off the Childhood Cancer Summit. It honors the co-chairs of Congress's Childhood Cancer Caucus.

Hard Time What I call my two and a half years from diagnosis to remission. It was scary and horrible and painful, but it's also when I got closer to my family and met a whole ton of angels.

Heparin A blood thinning drug. In my case, it kept blood clots from clogging up my PICC and port.

Inpatient A person who is stuck in the hospital.

Intake The part of a hospital that checks you in, draws your blood, checks your vitals, weight, and height, and then finds you an examining room—and a hospital room if you need it.

IV pole It looks the way it does in movies. It's metal, on wheels, and nurses hang bags of fluid on them. The fluid can be all kinds of things—medicine, nutrition, even blood. The fluid flows through a tube and into your body, through a port or a needle under your skin. It's like an annoying robot that follows you around. But it can be fun to stand on while your parents push you.

Kids v Cancer   A group started by Nancy Goodman, who lost her son Jacob to a kind of brain cancer called medulloblastoma. Her group did the big work in writing some of the most important childhood cancer bills, including the Creating Hope Act and the RACE for Children Act.

Lantana   My hometown, an hour outside of Dallas, Texas. It has the nicest people in the world, and it's right next door to ranch country.

Leucocytes   White blood cells, the soldiers that attack foreign invaders in your blood.

Leucovorin   Folinic acid. It can take away some of the side effects of methotrexate, like, I don't know, thinking you're having a stroke! The doctor gave me leucovorin, and my body stopped doing weird things. It worked.

Leukemia   Cancer in the parts of the body that make blood, such as your bone marrow. Most leukemia results from white blood cells that keep reproducing without stopping. White blood cells fight infection. You can't live without them. But with leukemia, the cells don't mature, and they don't work right. And they grow out of control. The most common kind of leukemia in kids is acute lymphocytic leukemia, or ALL. This kind of cancer has to do with the lymphatic system, vessels that carry fluid toward the heart. That's the kind of cancer I had.

Lobbyist   A person who tries to get Congress to pass a law. Anyone can be a lobbyist, including a kid. It helps to be part of an organization that can arrange visits.

Loophole   Something in a law that people or companies can get around. The Creating Hope Act had loopholes that excused drug companies from doing cancer research. It takes really smart lobbyists, activists, and members of Congress to close loopholes. Lawyers are really good at finding loopholes.

Lymphoma   Cancer in the cells called lymphocytes that help fight infections. I had friends who got lymphoma. It's awful.

Mays Family Foundation   Michael McCaul's wife, Linda, is on the board of directors of this foundation. Its money comes from Clear Channel, a company that owns lots of radio and television stations. Its website is maysfamilyfoundation.com.

Medulloblastoma   A kind of brain cancer. These tumors tend to spread to the other parts of the brain and to the spinal cord. This cancer is usually treated by surgery, radiation therapy, and chemotherapy.

Methotrexate   A drug that slows down the growth of cancer cells. I received this chemo three different ways during my two and a half years of chemo: in an oral pill, into my spine during spinal taps, and into my port. It can cause mouth sores, nausea, and liver damage. It gave me fevers every time I got it into my port, which meant I had to go to the ER every time... which was a LOT!

Migraine A terrible kind of headache. It was one of the side effects I got when I was in the hospital. They were caused by high blood pressure—another side effect of the steroid.

Milestone When a cancer kid gets past a stage, like getting out of the hospital or going into remission.

Miracle Something awesome that can't be explained by science or medicine. My blood count before surgery seemed like a miracle, though it could be that my short bit of transfusion did the job. I say miracle.

MRI Magnetic resonance imaging. You can see why medical people use abbreviations for everything. The MRI takes amazing pictures of your inside, just like a CT scan. The MRI can show some things that a CT scan can't, especially some types of cancer. But the machine is no fun. It's really really loud, with these giant clicks so you have to wear ear protection. And you're shut up inside this tube for what seems like hours, even though it's usually no more than 40 minutes. But during those 40 minutes you're not allowed to move. At all.

National Institutes of Health The main government agency that runs and funds medical research.

Neuroblastoma A kind of cancer that forms in certain types of nerve tissue. It is most common in babies and is the third most common type of cancer after leukemia and brain cancers.

Neurologist A doctor who solves problems with the nervous system, including the brain and spinal cord.

A neurologist figured out why I couldn't lift a chicken nugget or say the word "remember."

Neurotoxicity Neuro means nerves, and toxicity means poison. You do the math. My medicine to fight my cancer, methotrexate, messed up my brain for a while. That's what neurotoxicity is: a medicine or poison that messes up your nervous system. It can seem like you're having a stroke, or you can go into seizures. But doctors know how to treat neurotoxicity from methotrexate. See what I wrote about leucovorin.

No Poke Zone What I wrote on the window of my hospital room when I got sick of all the needles, pokes and prods. I wrote it small so the nurses and doctors who were doing all that horrible stuff to me couldn't see it. Even when I was most upset with them, I knew they were doing all they could to save my life.

Nurse You know what a nurse is. But there are many kinds. Some go to nursing school for two years, some for four years, and many have master's degrees, which means they get extra years of education after college. Some nurses even have Ph.D.'s, which makes them doctors of nursing. While most nurses are women, more and more are men. They are all angels!

Oncologist A cancer doctor. My brother, Grant, wants to be one. Oncologists save lives, and they also have to deal with really scared patients and families. My oncologist is one of the most amazing people I have ever met. She is super smart, like a really kind scientist.

Outpatient A fighter who goes to the cancer clinic for chemo and then gets to go home.

Oval Office The office of the President of the United States. It really is shaped like an oval, and it's bright and cheerful and has lots of windows. A nice place to work.

Packing What you do with a deep wound like what I had with my port. It's a kind of dressing, really light material that soaks up the juices in the wound and help you heal from the inside out. That way, the germs don't get trapped inside, which is what would happen if the wound healed from the skin down.

Pediatrician A doctor who works with kids and teenagers. The word comes from Greek, meaning "healer of children." Exactly. A pediatrician practices pediatrics, care of children.

Phlebotomist A person whose job it is to draw your blood—sticking you with a needle and taking it from your veins (or sometimes someplace else). My phlebotomist, Fatima, is a really close friend. She wears red scrubs and is good at distracting kids so they're not scared.

Photo Party Every year before Christmas, a bunch of volunteers come to our house, and we lay out the thousands of presents people donate to Sadie's Sleigh. They take up the entire cul-de-sac we live on. Then a photographer gets on a ladder and takes a picture. We have to box everything back up after that. But meanwhile, we have a party. It's the funnest, most joyful day you can possibly have. Except maybe for Christmas itself.

PICC   Peripherally inserted central catheter. It's a thin tube stuck with a needle under your skin so the medicine can come into your body. I got a PICC line after my port got infected.

Platelet   A tiny blood cell that clumps together with other platelets to stop bleeding. The clump is called a blood clot. When one of your blood vessels gets injured, platelets rush to that spot and plug it up. A low platelet count, which I had early in my treatment, is a very bad thing, because you can bleed to death inside.

Porch pirate   Someone who steals packages from people's porches and then sneaks off. What happened with Sadie's Sleigh was the opposite. People left packages on our porch and snuck off. These weren't pirates. They were elves.

Port   A kind of socket that a surgeon puts in your body so you don't have to get poked every time you need medicine. My port site got infected, so the doctors had to take it out again. Once it healed, I got another one put in. I still have this amazing scar that looks like I got shot. I love my scars.

Prognosis   A prediction of how well you're going to recover. Like a lot of medical words, it comes from a kind of Greek that hasn't been spoken by real people for thousands of years. In the old days, doctors used to study Greek, and it seemed cool to use Greek words to show how educated they were. "Pro" means before. The second part means "know." So prognosis means to "know before." Like, predict.

Propofol   The main anesthesia used on me. Like Versed, it makes you forget what happened to you. Its nickname is milk of amnesia, which is a joke about forgetting things. I got Propofol the 19 times I had a spinal tap, and I hated it every time.

RACE for Children Act   Research to Accelerate Cures and Equity. It's a law that helps bring money and attention to finding medicine for childhood cancer. I helped lobby for it with Kids v Cancer. Nancy Goodman wrote the bill. It passed and got signed by the President in 2017.

Radiologist   A doctor who's an expert in looking inside your body and figuring out what's going on. She uses all kinds of expensive machines, including CT and MRI, along with other technology like positron emission tomography (don't ask me), fusion imaging (again, don't ask), and ultrasound.

Rally to the U.S. Capitol   The biggest event at CureFest, when thousands of people march up to the Capitol in Washington, D.C. Tattoo Tom leads the way. I'm usually in the front with him and my family.

Reauthorization   I didn't know this, but some laws like the Creating Hope Act expire, meaning they stop being laws after a few years. It's called a sunset clause. Which means you have to lobby and get it passed all over again. We're hoping that the Creating Hope Act becomes permanent.

Red blood cell   This is what carries oxygen around your body. Weird fact: More than three quarters of all the cells in your body are red blood cells. And these cells make up almost half your blood.

Remission When you're in remission, the doctors can't find any cancer cells. But wait. Doesn't that mean you're cured? There's always a chance that cancer cells are hiding somewhere in your body. To be cured, there has to be no cancer—and no chance that that cancer will come back somehow. I'm in remission, which means I still go in for regular checkups to make sure no cancer cells are hiding and show up again.

Rhabdoid tumor A kind of kidney cancer when it's malignant.

Roid rage The feeling some people get when they take steroids. It makes them angry. My version of roid rage was just crying. I don't like to upset people.

Rotunda The dome in the Capitol. It's amazing, like a giant church dedicated to democracy.

Ryan Seacrest Studio A real studio in ten hospitals across the country, including my hospital in Dallas. You see Ryan Seacrest on TV all the time—*American Idol*, *Live with Kelly & Ryan*; he hosts all kinds of shows. He's also a clothing designer. But I think his studios are the most amazing thing he does. Kids can record TV and radio programs and create Web videos, and it's really professional. The radio and TV shows get broadcast to the TV sets in the hospital. Big stars come to perform. And the studios put out shows made by local journalism students. You can see whether there's a studio in your hospital by going to ryanseacrestfoundation.org.

Sadie Keller Foundation My foundation! At sadie-kellerfoundation.org, you can see parts of videos I've made through the years. And you can see how to help other kids with cancer, by giving money or toys or setting up Sadie's Sleigh in your own city. Mom runs the foundation with a few amazing people.

Sadie on a Stick My picture on stiff board, mounted on a stick so kids who get Milestone Gifts can take a selfie with me. When the family posts the picture on social media, more people hear about Sadie's Sleigh, and that brings in even more gifts for kids.

Sadie's Sleigh That's my program for giving presents to kids who have to be in the hospital on Christmas. We call it Sadie's Sleigh, but hundreds of people make it happen every year. "Hundreds of People's Sleigh" just wouldn't sound right.

Saline syringe It looks like something that would have a needle on the end of it for getting a shot. But it's just used to squirt saline—salt water—through a catheter or PICC. It flushes junk out of the line, keeping it clean.

Scrubs The uniforms all the medical people wear. They're called scrubs because people have to wear them in a scrubbed—really really clean—environment like a hospital. The first scrubs were green. Some history types say they were green because that color is as far as you can get from red, which reminds people of blood. This is funny, since these days in my hospital the phlebotomists, the people who draw your blood, wear red. Most medical people don't own their scrubs.

The hospital owns or rents them, and that way they can be sure the scrubs are sterile every day. There's a whole industry for scrubs now, with scrub fashions.

Side effects The ways that drugs make you sick. If you're a cancer kid, your doctor will give printed side effect lists for every drug they give you. My cancer treatments made me sick. I had almost every side effect on the list. And some that weren't even on the list. But the drugs saved my life. Worth it.

Social worker In a hospital, the social worker works with the family to help them cope with all the problems of having someone really sick. Our social worker, Jennifer, even helped my parents with paperwork.

Speaker of the House The most powerful member of Congress, and third in line for the presidency if anything happens to the President and Vice President.

Spinal fluid The big name for this is cerebrospinal fluid, meaning it's in both your brain and your spinal cord. Your body has about two-thirds of a cup of this liquid. It keeps your brain and spine from bumping around, carries stuff you need from the blood, and gets rid of junk from your brain. Spinal fluid can tell doctors whether you have leukemia. They take a tablespoon or so of the liquid by sticking a long needle into your back. I was asleep, under anesthesia, when my doctor did this to me.

Spinal tap A procedure where fluid gets pulled out of your spine so it can be tested. Also, for me, methotrexate chemo was put into my spine.

Spine The bones that go up your back. But the spine is more than bones. In the middle is the spinal cord, a tube that goes from your head all the way down to your lower back. It carries nerve signals from the brain down your body. For instance, when you touch something hot, your hand pulls back before you can even tell yourself, "Wow, that's hot!" That was your brain shooting the signal down your spinal cord right to your arm. The spinal cord also contains spinal fluid. Doctors take a bit of that fluid out to measure how much leukemia you have.

St. Baldrick's A foundation that raises millions and millions of dollars to help close the funding gap for cures for kids with cancer. It's called St. Baldrick's because people raise money by getting their heads shaved on St. Patrick's Day. The foundation raises money in other ways, too. I love their website, stbaldricks.org.

STAR Act A law I lobbied for. It stands for Survivorship, Treatment, Access, and Research. It gives money and encourages drug companies to come up with treatments that help kids survive cancer. And it also lets scientists share their discoveries.

Stem cell transplant This is when medical people take cells out of your blood or bone marrow and turn them into useful things in your body. Stem cells are amazing. The embryonic, or baby, stem cells can be turned into all kinds of cures.

Steroid A kind of drug that fights inflammation, which is what happens when white blood cells fight enemies in the body. The steroid dexamethasone is important for treating cancer, but also makes you feel terrible.

StillBrave   A foundation started by my friend Tattoo Tom Mitchell. His daughter, Shayla, died of Hodgkin's lymphoma, a kind of cancer, when Tom was a single dad. He has a cool website, stillbrave.org.

Strep throat   A really bad infection in the throat and the tonsils that hits a lot of kids. It's treated with antibiotics. I got it when cancer screwed up my immune system—before we knew I had cancer.

Stroke   This is when the blood gets cut off from the brain, usually when an artery gets blocked. Like, a plumbing problem. Without blood, brain cells don't get the oxygen and food they need, and they start dying. You can feel tingly in your arm or leg, have trouble speaking, all kinds of things. You need to get to the ER right away. A CT scan will tell the doctors whether you're having a stroke. I had a lot of symptoms of stroke. But the CT scan showed it wasn't a stroke. I was having a reaction to getting methotrexate in my spine. Of all the side effects I got, this one was the scariest. Every side effect was a test—of me, of my family, and of Dr. Engel. It was a kind of test where you don't know how many questions you're going to have to answer. You take the test, and you pass, and then your body says, "Wait. We're not done." Life is that kind of test, right? Except that my treatment and side effects were a test that was way speeded up.

Survivorship   In cancer, they don't usually say you're cured. They say you survive. It can mean you have no sign of cancer, or just that you're still alive. There's always a chance that the cancer can come back, which is why survivors have to keep going in for checkups. Here's an amazing number: In America, there are more than 15,500,000 people who have had cancer and are still alive. That includes adults as well as kids.

Syringe   What nurses and doctors use when they poke you. The syringe holds the medicine, which goes through a needle at the end.

T cell   Hunter cells in your body that go after anything they think is foreign. T cells are white blood cells. In some cases, the T cells are the cancer cells.

Tegaderm   A see-through dressing that sticks to your skin like a Band-Aid. It helped keep my port in place, but also gave me an allergic rash.

The Truth 365   A campaign that uses films and videos to raise awareness for childhood cancer. The organization's Mr. Mike—Mike Gillette— put me in some of his videos and recommended me to Kids v Cancer, which made me a lobbyist. You really should see the cool website with tons of photos and videos, thetruth365.org, and their Facebook page.

Therapy   Treatment that makes you better. Childhood cancer therapy comes in all kinds. What made me better was chemotherapy, meaning therapy using chemicals. Drugs, in other words. Other kinds of cancer therapy include surgery, radiation, stem cell transplant, and immunotherapy. This last one is the newest kind, where doctors use your own body's disease fighters to fight cancer. CAR-T is a kind of immunotherapy.

Tylenol   A drug that helps with pain or lessens a fever. It can also make you feel better when you have an allergic reaction. When the nurse gave me Benadryl for my allergic reaction to platelets, she also gave me Tylenol. The medical name for the drug that makes Tylenol work is acetaminophen. I'm telling you this because you might hear medical people use that word.

Versed   A drug that makes you comfortable during a medical procedure like surgery—and then makes you forget everything that happened during the procedure.

Vincristine   The main medicine my doctor used to fight my cancer. It's a drug that stops the cancer cell from splitting itself into two cells, which is how the cancer spreads. Vincristine says stop. That's what it does. It made my hair fall out for all two and a half years (another weird, rare Sadie side effect), and it also gave me terrible jaw pain.

Vitals   Vital signs. These are things that medical people like doctors and nurses watch for to make sure you're okay. The vital signs include heart rate, respiratory (breathing) rate, blood pressure, oxygen saturation, respiratory effort, capillary refill time (how fast the color returns in your finger after it's been squeezed), and temperature. When you're in the hospital, you'll see a nurse wheeling a computer cart into your room. She's checking your vitals against what they were before. Plus, she's recording medications and things like that.

White blood cell   Your body's frontline soldier. White cells make up only one percent of your blood, but they go running when they hear about a virus or bacteria or some other foreign enemy. A low white cell count can make you get sick really easily. That was part of my problem.

Wilms tumor   A kind of kidney cancer. My friend Vara had it.

Yellow Ball   A huge party we throw every year in Dallas to make money for the Sadie Keller Foundation.

Zofran   A drug that keeps you from throwing up. It's probably one reason I never threw up during the Hard Time. Thank God!

#SadieStrong   My own personal hashtag, which I use on Facebook and Instagram. It means what it says.

#yougotthisgirl   This became my slogan and the hashtag I used on social media during my treatment. It made me feel like I could do anything.